WELCOME TO HELL

WELCOME TO HELL

Colin Martin

PUBLISHED BY MAVERICK HOUSE PUBLISHERS.

Maverick House, Office 19, Dunboyne Business Park,
Dunboyne, Co. Meath, Ireland.
Maverick House Asia, Level 43, United Center, 323 Silom Road,
Bangrak, Bangkok 10500, Thailand.

http://www.maverickhouse.com
info@maverickhouse.com

ISBN: 978-0-954870-77-5 (0-9548707-7-8)

Copyright for text © Colin Martin, 2005
Copyright for typesetting, editing, layout, design
© Maverick House Publishers

This edition reprinted 2008.

15

DEDICATION

I'd like to dedicate this book to everybody that helped me during the eight years I was in prison but especially to John Mulcahy and John Kealy. I wouldn't have made it without them.

Prologue

My name is Colin Martin, but that's not so important.
What is important is what happened to me and what
you're about to read – because it could easily have
been you.

I've just been released from Lard Yao prison in
Bangkok. I was jailed there for murder, but I was not
guilty.

I was attacked by a man who was trying to kill me,
so I fought back to save my life. Who wouldn't? The
next thing I knew, the man was dead and I was in jail.

You've probably heard horror stories of life in a
Thai jail. So had I. When I was first sent to prison, I
asked one of my fellow prisoners, a Swiss guy called
Bruno, if it was really that bad. It couldn't be as bad as
they made it out, could it?

Bruno gave a dry laugh.

'Welcome to hell,' he said.

I spent eight years in jail, and I can tell you, hell is no exaggeration. It depends on what your concept of hell is. This experience was every bit as bad as I imagine hell to be. I shouldn't have been in prison in the first place. I was tortured by police until I made a false confession.

Once in prison, I was beaten endlessly by the guards. I went for days without eating because the food was so revolting. I was forced to wear shackles on my legs for two years. I almost died from tuberculosis which the prison officials left untreated.

I saw things nobody should have to see.

I saw prisoners murdered. I saw prisoners rape each other.

It was a living nightmare – one I couldn't wake myself up from.

Some memories of what happened are clearer in my mind than others. One in particular stands out.

On my first day at the prison, I was stripped naked and searched along with the other new prisoners. There were about 15 of us, lined up in a row. Another 100 or so existing prisoners were there watching.

A guard singled one of the new prisoners out – and told him to masturbate.

'What?' the guy said.

'Masturbate, and do it now!'

The guy just stood there, as shocked as I was.

'Dear God,' I thought. 'What kind of a prison is this?'

Three quick, hard jabs with the guard's baton, and the poor guy lifted his penis and started to masturbate. I knew that if he ordered me to do that there was going to be a problem. I would smash the bastard in the mouth.

Thankfully, he didn't, and moved on.

The commando started walking back and forth along the line of new prisoners.

'You think you're Mafia. You think you're tough. You think you're big men,' he said. 'You're not. I am the boss here!'

He walked on, pounding his chest.

'I'm the boss, and you *will* obey me. If I tell you to shit, you *will* shit! Nobody fucks with me. Fuck with me and you die!'

I believed him. Anyone who was sadistic enough to humiliate a man by making him masturbate in front of 100 prisoners was a sick bastard, and capable of getting his kicks by killing someone just as easily.

The Thai justice system is brutal, but it's also a big business. In any way they possibly can, the cops, lawyers, guards and prison directors will cheat you out of your money.

When I was first arrested, I was told that if I paid 300,000 baht (around US $12,000) I'd be released. If I'd paid, I would have walked free. But I didn't have the money, so I went to prison. It was as simple as that.

I now know there have been many cases like mine.

In Thailand, you don't even have to commit a crime to find yourself in prison. Sometimes they'll bang you up because there's a chance you'll be able to pay them a few baht – or because you can't. You just have to be in the wrong place at the wrong time.

I'll give you an example.

Kevin, an Englishman, was on his way home after a night out and stopped off for a last beer before bed. While sitting in the bar, he was propositioned by a prostitute. He declined her services.

Five minutes later she returned – with a cop in tow. She accused Kevin of stealing her cigarettes. Kevin was searched and no cigarettes were found. As this lady was in some distress over the loss of her cigarettes, Kevin was duly asked to pay 3,000 baht to sort the problem out.

He refused. He hadn't taken the cigarettes and, even if he had, a packet of cigarettes is only worth 30 baht.

Kevin was arrested, charged with theft, and sent to jail.

After two weeks of prison, he paid.

It's always worst for foreigners. If there's ever a dispute between a Thai and a foreigner, the foreigner will be the one arrested. It's not that the cops take the Thai's side or that they dislike foreigners.

I gradually came to understand that it's about money.

Foreigners have it, Thais don't. For the cops, there's no point in arresting a Thai. He doesn't have any money. The cop will always arrest the foreigner because he can pay. And chances are, after a day or two in the Thai justice system, he will.

In Thailand, justice is simply a matter of mathematics.

1

My life has been far from average. But before this nightmare began, that's exactly what it was. I was an ordinary businessman, and I led a perfectly normal life.

My family originally came from County Monaghan in Ireland but moved to Liverpool to secure work. They were an average working-class family: not rich, not poor.

My father, Tommy Senior, started out as a bread man. He delivered bread around the working-class estates of Merseyside, but he eventually got himself qualified as a welder and worked in the shipyards and factories for a few years.

He left Liverpool after being offered work on some new factories, and eventually he ended up working on nuclear power plants.

My mother's name was Maisie. As was traditional in those days, she stayed at home and looked after her children.

I was the third of five. My sister Mary was the eldest, followed by my brother Tommy. Then there were my younger brothers Brendan and Paul.

We had a relatively privileged childhood. When I was six years old my parents bought their first house in Manchester where we lived through most of my school years. During this time my father went away to work in Saudi Arabia, in Algeria and throughout Europe.

He was a driven man. Eventually, with his best friend, he opened his own company, Martin and Goodwin, which contracted work for construction machinery.

Like most Irish emigrants, my parents kept in close touch with our extended family in Ireland. We used to go to Ireland every year for our holidays, as most Irish families did.

I suppose my parents had always dreamed of returning to Ireland and opening their own business at home.

This dream eventually came true for them in 1975 when they bought a pub in Carrickmacross in County Monaghan.

That summer, we all packed up and moved to Ireland. My father sold his share of the partnership with Tony Goodwin, and bought what was then called Murray's pub.

While my father and mother got on with the daily business of running the pub, we kids took the town by storm – especially the boys. I was about 15 years old but I settled very quickly in Carrickmacross.

Despite moving houses and cities a few times, all in all, I'd say that most of my youth was normal.

* * *

It was the career path I followed that led me to Thailand. After I left school I went to England and worked on building sites for a few years, and at Heathrow Airport for a while. There were no jobs in Ireland at the time. Many young people emigrated in order to find work.

I eventually got a job as an apprentice pipe fitter.

As part of my training I had to learn the basics of welding. Anything I built would have to be welded. I have to admit that I'd never wanted to follow my father into welding. In fact, it was the last thing I wanted to do, so I was really shocked to find out that I was actually very good at it.

I worked for various companies over the next few years, and at 21 I was given a chance to go and work offshore on the oil rigs and pipeline barges in the North Sea.

This was mostly seasonal work, six or seven months per year during the good weather. In the winter months the North Sea is too rough to lay any pipelines, so I'd be at home for a good part of the year. At home, I'd study and take courses.

After some four years I finally made it to the position of a pipeline welder, which isn't easy. These welders are regarded as the best in the world and the competition for work is fierce.

A pipeline welder is allowed zero mistakes, and zero defects. Every single weld must be 100 per cent X-rayed and tested. If too many of your welds fail the tests, you're fired. With the costs involved in laying a pipeline, there isn't any room for error.

I earned a lot of money and made a lot of good friends during the years I worked offshore but, when my son Jason was born, I quit. My own father had worked away from home during my childhood and I didn't want to miss my children growing up.

I'd met Jason's mother, Paula, a couple of years previously, and we'd been going steady. Paula was from Crossmaglen in South Armagh, just over the border in Northern Ireland.

We decided not to rush into marriage and it wasn't until three years later, when she was pregnant with my second son Carl, that we decided to tie the knot.

When my son Jason was born, I worked around the local area – in Dundalk, Castleblayney, and Newry, as well as in Dublin.

But there wasn't really that much money for welders in Ireland at that time, so I was forced to start working in Europe – in countries like Holland, Belgium and Germany.

This caused tensions at home. My wife used to hate the telephone ringing, because it usually meant that someone was offering me a job somewhere.

Sometimes I'd go as a welder, sometimes as a foreman and sometimes as a supervisor. Sometimes I wouldn't go at all. It all depended on the money and how badly I needed it. If the money was right, I'd be on the plane in the morning. As I say, my wife hated the phone ringing.

I firmly believed in making as much money as possible while I was young. Sometimes the more experience and skill you had under your belt the harder it was to get work.

My attitude has always been to make money while I was still physically fit enough to do it.

I was never interested in a nine-to-five job. A guy can give 20 years of his life to a company, but if there's a problem or no work he's out the door, just like everyone else. I wasn't interested in that. I have always worked for me.

I performed a service; a company employed me and paid for that service, but if the money wasn't good enough or I didn't like the terms, I'd go and work for somebody else.

This principle stood by me. It allowed me to travel and encouraged me to build my own business.

* * *

I ended up working in Holland as a self-employed supervisor. Companies would hire me to supervise their construction projects or to advise on them. Sometimes they would ask me for extra manpower and I'd try and find the people they needed.

After a year or so of this, I decided to open my own company and to supply manpower directly. So, shortly after I married Paula, I moved the family over to Holland.

I opened my own company, and called it Spectac Welding and Construction (Holland). It was a difficult move.

The company mostly supplied manpower services to the construction industry. If times were hard, I would work as a welder to make ends meet, but my heart was always in the company.

We were a happy family. My wife was happy with the move to Holland. My son Jason learnt Dutch and attended a private school. My second son Carl was still too young for school, but it wasn't long before he was joined at home by a sister – Nicole.

We were an average family making our way in the world. I had my fair share of ups and downs, but Spectac eventually got established and became a profitable company. I was a contented man.

* * *

I spent a lot of my time looking for new contracts, because once one job finished the workers would become free, and I'd need somewhere new to place them.

I noticed an advertisement in the Dutch press in the summer of 1994. It was from a company based in Thailand called Offshore Construction Services – OCS. I assumed at the time that this was a legitimate firm, but was to discover later that the name had been either hi-jacked, stolen or made up by a group of fraudsters.

In this advertisement they explained that there was a severe shortage of trained engineering personnel in

Asia, and they were trying to interest any European companies with skills in this area.

At first I didn't take much notice. I thought the advert was aimed at larger construction companies. OCS wouldn't be interested in doing business with a small company like mine.

A couple of months later this advertisement appeared again. This time when I read it I thought, 'What the hell?'

I sent off a letter of introduction and a prospectus, which outlined the type of services and personnel we could supply. I didn't know if OCS would reply, but it was worth a shot.

After a month or so, I received a reply from OCS stating that they were impressed with the quality of our personnel and would like a meeting to discuss this further.

I was delighted. A contract with a big company like that would really help build my reputation. I flew to Thailand straight away.

No one told me that Bangkok was the crime capital of Asia. My knowledge of the city was superficial. I knew nothing of the Thai black market and the implicit dangers involved in operating there. In time I would learn that Bangkok was a city where everything had its price. I was oblivious to the fact that money laundering and organized crime were the lifeblood of the Thai economy. While blood letting between gangs was rare, Bangkok had a dark and dangerous underbelly that visitors seldom see. By the time I arrived there, organised crime had discovered the attractions of the city and its corrupt authorities. The city had become a haven for all sorts of criminals. If I'd known there was a large foreign criminal fraternity at work in Bangkok, I wouldn't have travelled there. I always thought that Bangkok was an easy-going kind of place. But it wasn't – that was my fatal mistake.

Bangkok, conveniently wedged between South and East Asia and boasting a well developed transport and communications infrastructure, made an ideal venue for gangs who wanted to do a little networking, organise drug deals or diversify into elaborate frauds. These mobsters mingled with Bangkok's large expatriate business community and the army of Chinese, Taiwanese, Russians, Koreans, Europeans, Nigerians, Colombians, Australians and New Zealanders. They dressed up as businessmen and sometimes investors, and many of the criminals were long-time residents. These criminals controlled the black market and were responsible for fraud in the region. They could arrange anything.

If they weren't dealing in heroin, they produced counterfeit goods and clothes. Brands such as Nike, Polo, Lacoste, Christian Dior and Microsoft were mass produced by fakers in factories across the city. The Thais were so good that they even started faking pharmaceutical products, fake cigarettes and alcohol. They could even make bogus computer parts. These criminals were immune from prosecution because of slow court procedures and under-the-table payments to friendly police officers who turned a blind eye. Crime mingled like a virus in the blood-stream of Bangkok. I know this now, but back then I was completely blind to the dangers of the Far East.

I couldn't get lost in Bangkok now if I tried but I was like a lot of first-time visitors when I first arrived. Although I had travelled across several countries, I had never seen anything like it. I have to admit that I was overcome by the sheer volume of people living there. The airport seemed manic; it was a sea of people. There were people everywhere, all shouting and jostling past each other. But I remember the heat more than anything else.

As I travelled to my hotel the afternoon I arrived, my clothes began to dampen with sweat. I never experienced heat like it. Bangkok's average daytime temperature is very rarely much below 30 degrees centigrade at any time of year, and the night-time temperature is not much cooler. But there was no sun; the sky that day was grey and overcast. The heat, combined with the humidity and pollution that hung in the air, made it almost impossible to breathe.

I also recall being struck by the city's expanse: the endless high-rise buildings, the busy expressway flyovers and what I can only describe as the commotion. Bangkok city intimidated and fascinated me.

Prostitutes stood on every street corner. There were people everywhere. There was no free space. There were billboards of western companies advertising in English, yet you only needed to look a little under the surface to see it was Asian.

In between the skyscrapers, there were Temples and Spirit Houses built for good luck alongside almost every major building. The place was alive. I saw a file of Buddhist monks making their way through the traffic with an elephant.

Even the traffic was overwhelming. As I sat in the taxi, I found myself trapped in a permanent traffic jam, which my driver called a *rot dtit*. Jammed traffic is a fact of life in Bangkok. Simple journeys that should take 20 minutes end up taking over an hour, even out side of rush hour.

Thai people rarely walk any significant distance; which has led to an explosion in cars, buses, taxis and *tuk-tuks* – a traditional form of transport consisting of a carriage pulled by bicycle. But these only accumulated to make the traffic jams and pollution worse.

The combined effect of the traffic, heat, humidity, noise, dirt, pollution and the unappealing look of the city made me want to leave Bangkok almost as soon as I'd arrived. I couldn't wait to reach the sanctuary of my hotel, which I knew would have air-conditioning. But part of me admired the city and my interest was aroused. As I checked into my hotel that afternoon, I remember thinking that this was a city full of opportunities.

I was picked up at my hotel by a man from OCS who introduced himself as Ronnie Hayes. He was Australian, in his late fifties, slim, about six foot (the same height as me) with a shock of grey hair.

He was dressed in a sharp suit – probably designer, I thought – and he wore a lot of gold jewellery. A bit flashy for my taste, but he pulled it off.

Hayes said he was head of the engineering department. We had lunch and arranged to meet at the OCS office the next morning in downtown Bangkok. It was only later that I discovered this was a false name.

The offices were as you'd expect – busy and professional, with about 15 secretaries and other office personnel working at computer stations and going about their daily business.

I was introduced to the personnel officer, the offshore co-ordinator, the accounts officer and to Gerald O'Connor, the company's managing director.

O'Connor was five foot seven, and built like a rugby player. He was much younger than Hayes, in his late thirties – about my age, in fact.

We had a productive meeting and discussed safety qualifications, work permits, schedules, and planning.

I had over eight years' experience working offshore and Spectac already had some highly qualified offshore workers, so nothing that was discussed would have been too difficult for us. It was proposed that in all, Spectac would supply 250 men to various OCS projects with a relief crew of another 250 men for the changeover every month.

I left Bangkok thinking I had secured the deal.

OCS promised to contact me after they had their own internal discussions. Obviously they would have other interested companies to consider.

During our discussions, O'Connor has said that Spectac would have to be accepted by his head office in Chicago, USA. I thought nothing more of the talks but was quietly confident.

About two or three weeks later I received a fax from OCS inviting me back to Thailand to discuss some design drawing.

The meeting went well and I was told that OCS were very interested in using Spectac. I went home once more with high hopes.

* * *

Some weeks later in October, I received another fax. I was invited to Thailand once more to discuss more construction plans. The fax I received hinted at a positive reaction from the firm's head office in Chicago. I was excited, and flew over.

When I arrived, I was told the decision was indeed positive. The OCS office in Chicago was very impressed by the range of services we were offering. However, they said, I was going to have to fill out quite an amount of paperwork.

If OCS were to offer Spectac a contract, they said they would be put to considerable expense. Each man would require a medical certificate of fitness, an offshore survival certificate, an offshore work permit, a welding qualification, and a permit to work in Thailand.

They would also have to pay insurance, return air fares, and hotel bills. While waiting for these permits, nobody is allowed to set foot offshore, or do any kind of work, and you have to be in Thailand to get them – which takes a minimum of two weeks.

Because of the expense, OCS were concerned that firstly, the personnel would be experienced enough to get through all of the necessary red tape, and that secondly, these workers would stay for the duration of the contract. If they left halfway through the contract, said OCS, they would have to be replaced, causing delays and more expense.

In view of this, we would have to make some sort of commitment. OCS insisted that Spectac should pay what they described as an 'integrity bond' of US $100,000.

This would ensure that we would only supply them with experienced and qualified personnel. Obviously, we would lose this bond if we couldn't supply experienced workers who could get the required certificates and permits.

Furthermore, each worker would have to pay his own integrity bond of US $12,000, to make sure he'd stay for the duration of the contract.

OCS said that if Spectac were to pay this, it would mean nothing to the actual workforce. They wouldn't care about the company losing a bond, but if they had to pay one themselves they would be sure to think twice before simply quitting.

The $100,000 for Spectac was my responsibility, but I couldn't answer for the workers. I could only tell OCS that I would have to put it to them, and ask them whether they would be prepared or be able to pay this bond.

I knew it was going to be a problem, but OCS were adamant. I offered to double Spectac's own integrity bond, but they wouldn't accept that. It wouldn't necessarily hold the workers to their contracts, they said.

After many lengthy discussions I was able to get OCS to accept that the workers, if they agreed at all, would have their bond returned over the course of the contract and not at the end.

The men would pay the bond, but it would be returned quarterly in four payments of $3,000. That was the best I could do. I figured once we had proved that our workforce was what we had promised, then we could try and get the bond cancelled or, at the very least, reduced.

I wasn't happy about having to pay any kind of bond, but I did a little checking and in Asia it seems that asking for a bond of some kind before hiring someone isn't so unusual. Not all companies do it, but there are a lot who insist. After all, it sort of made sense.

I returned to Holland and held a staff meeting. The original contract was to be for one year to build a crane barge, but OCS had told us that if Spectac performed as promised, then they might consider us for several other projects, totalling 500 men.

I didn't have $100,000 in cash reserves, so I had to borrow from my bank.

Meanwhile, my lawyer worked out a guarantee, which I inserted into the contract. OCS would pay an amount equal to the total of the bonds into a nominated bank, which would act as guarantor.

OCS in Thailand agreed, but they'd have to clear it with Chicago. However, this would only be a formality.

OCS offered Spectac a preliminary contract, with a full and proper contract to be signed once approval came through. The starting date was 1 December, which I thought was a little close to Christmas for the men to be so far away from home. They argued that the men would have to be on hand a couple of weeks before the actual start-up date at the end of December or the beginning of January.

The ball was now in my court. I'd now have to find workers who were willing to pay the integrity bond.

I looked first amongst our own workers, but I also placed an advert in the Dutch press. The response I received was good, but when a lot of the workers were told about the integrity bond, they immediately lost interest.

Nobody liked the idea of these bonds, but once I explained in detail about the reasons for them and the fact that they would be returned quarterly, most of the men began to see that OCS had a point.

I didn't like the bond clause either, but OCS weren't giving me any choice. The full integrity bond would have to be paid. I managed to get 30 workers willing to start working on the project.

I liked to think of myself as a shrewd businessman. Since my first dealings with OCS, I had done a little discreet checking.

I established that OCS was a registered company. I even confirmed that they had offices in Chicago and New York. In their offices, the lease, telephone etc were all registered under OCS. The drawings were also genuine construction drawings.

I'd even taken the chance and sent a copy of Gerald O'Connor's passport to the Irish embassy in Kuala Lumpur, Malaysia, who confirmed it to be genuine.

Without going to the extreme of hiring private detectives to check O'Connor and Hayes, there wasn't much more that I could do, or at least do discreetly. All of the checks I made came back positive.

* * *

The day arrived and Spectac was ready to send the workers to Asia. All we needed was Chicago's approval.

I eventually received a fax from OCS telling me that the contract had been cleared by Chicago. They now wanted Spectac to mobilise the men, and fly them over to Thailand.

The next morning I received another fax. It said that OCS had now fulfilled their part of the agreement and were under pressure from head office to 'get some bodies on the job'.

OCS had given Spectac an opportunity of continuous work, they said. They had fulfilled every agreement. Now if Spectac was interested in doing business with them, they wanted the integrity bonds paid and the men on site. Every day we delayed cost OCS hundreds of thousands of dollars in production loss, fees and expenses.

This fax surprised me. Spectac had only held off because we were waiting for the contract to be finalised by OCS. I thought this was a strange way to conduct business. The tone of all their communications was aimed at getting Spectac to lodge cash to cover the integrity bonds in the trustee account.

OCS had proposed an obscure bank somewhere in Polynesia to act as guarantor. As a final check, I asked my own bank about it. They told me yes, this place exists and yes, it would be common for big companies to use this kind of small clearing bank for tax purposes.

Although my bank hadn't talked with the Polynesian bank yet because of time differences, I wasn't unduly concerned. They were working on it, though, and would get back to me in a day or two with the result.

I didn't want to upset OCS, but I had to verify the Polynesian bank. On the other hand, OCS were waiting for our response and complaining about delays.

A decision had to be made one way or the other. Did we go? Or did we pull out of the contract? Somebody always has to make that final decision, and I made it as director of Spectac. I ordered Spectac's integrity bond of $100,000 be paid immediately.

2

I decided to fly with the first group of men to Thailand. That way, if any problems came up, I would be on hand to deal with them.

I contacted the men and told them that they should be ready to go in two groups of 15. The first group would travel with me and the second group would follow a few days later. 30 men travelling in one group would be just too much, between flights, baggage, taxis and hotels. Everybody said they were ready, and had the $12,000.

I arranged for everybody to meet at Schiphol Airport in Amsterdam, and fly together from there to Bangkok.

On the day in question, I waited at Schiphol with Spectac's personnel manager, Hadawji. We gave out the tickets and contracts and checked the men's passports.

Everything was going smoothly until I asked the men for their integrity bonds. I wanted to collect all the money and declare it to customs as one amount.

I didn't want to have to go through 15 different declarations, or risk someone trying to smuggle their cash out.

I told the men to bring dollars because I didn't want any problems or delays because someone thought they were being clever with some foreign currency.

But it turned out that I had a much bigger problem.

Most of the men had lied. Out of the 15 only two or three had the full amount of money with them. Some had about half, others a few thousand. One of them had just $2,000.

To be honest, I just felt like walking out and going home. Screaming and shouting and jumping up and down wasn't going to do a bit of good. I was furious.

I'd listened to these men on the phone for weeks.

'No problem!' they'd said. 'I've got the money. When do we leave?'

Now here they were at the airport with blank faces and empty pockets.

I had two options. I could walk away, or I could try to sort something out.

I talked it over with Hadawji and we decided that just this once, Spectac would cover the difference for each man and deduct it later from his salary. After all, I had bought air tickets and made hotel reservations. If I cancelled them, it would probably cost Spectac just as much anyway.

The money was collected and signed for, and the men made their excuses. I heard lots of different excuses. Some said they just couldn't raise the money in time while others said they were afraid of losing it.

We sorted the money problem out just in time to catch our flight to Bangkok.

We landed in South East Asia the following afternoon.

Once everyone had settled in to their hotel rooms, I held a team meeting. I decided which of the men I would appoint as supervisors or foremen, and gave them all a few pointers about Thai culture.

I warned the men about the dangers of Bangkok and told them that people weren't always what they seemed. Thailand has a large number of the third gender, called *katoeys*, who can be very difficult to spot. I didn't want anybody taking his new found love up to his room and getting more than he'd bargained for. A lot of the men knew or had heard about these ladyboys – half man, half woman – but I thought I'd better explain it, just in case.

The following day, as arranged, Hayes came to meet me at the hotel. We spent a couple of hours going over the men's CVs.

I'd chosen the men carefully. They all had most of the paperwork themselves. I'd hoped that by providing all this, OCS could save time.

I also wanted to use this point to get OCS to reconsider asking for the integrity bonds. If the men were supplying all the documentation, OCS's actual costs would be cut to a work permit and insurance.

Their overheads would also be cut because the men wouldn't have to sit around waiting.

Hayes was impressed that Spectac was thinking ahead; he was sure O'Connor, his boss, would see things the same way. Of course, he told me they'd have to check that the Thai authorities would accept this paperwork, but he said it shouldn't be a problem.

O'Connor didn't come to that meeting but Hayes agreed to meet the men. They all had questions, which Hayes answered, and he laughed and joked with the men as the meeting went on.

After the meeting the men went off to do a little sightseeing.

I'd arranged with Hayes to meet with him and O'Connor the next morning. I wanted to hand over the money for the integrity bonds.

The next day, which was a Friday, only Hayes turned up.

He told me that O'Connor had to rush away to clear some technical problems on one of OCS's other projects. Hayes said that the bonds would have to be cleared that day so that the information and a copy of the receipt could be sent to OCS Chicago before the weekend. Otherwise there would be delays, and that wouldn't impress Chicago.

I explained that the original of the guarantee still hadn't been given to me and I would need it for our lawyers.

'No worries,' said Hayes. 'Gerry has the original. It's all signed and sealed.'

However, O'Connor wouldn't be back in Bangkok before the banks closed, Hayes explained. The money, nevertheless, would have to be cleared that day.

'Look,' said Hayes, 'Pay the money into the bank today. We'll get the paperwork off to Chicago. Then when Gerry gets back on Monday you can both sit down and iron out the details. You'll get your guarantee first thing on Monday morning. There won't be any problem with that.'

I had no reason not to trust them but this was all very unusual.

But then, they'd kept their promises so far.

I decided to throw caution to the wind and pay the money into the bank at closing time.

I remember it was a Friday so I thought that no withdrawal could be made until the following Monday morning. As far as I was concerned, the money was safe.

The second team arrived in Thailand the following Monday morning, as planned.

Hadawji called me to say she had met the men at Schiphol airport and once again only a small number had the full $12,000. As before, I told her to make up the difference from Spectac money.

Everything was running smoothly. On Tuesday morning I met Hayes and O'Connor.

They told me that my payment had been received by OCS in Chicago, who had given the green light to get started.

Next, O'Connor gave me a copy of the original bank guarantee. As promised, it was all signed and sealed. I read it through and it was the exact same as the one faxed to our offices.

I had the money for the last group's integrity bonds in my briefcase, because it had been arranged to go together to the bank after the men had been sent on their way.

O'Connor suggested that rather than leave the money at the hotel overnight again he could take it and lock it in the office safe. First thing in the morning he'd have his personal assistant rush it over to the bank.

That would mean putting a lot of trust in this man. But to be honest, the idea made a lot of sense. Why shouldn't I trust O'Connor?

I handed over the briefcase containing the cash and O'Connor wrote out a receipt. I didn't suspect a thing.

* * *

The truth was that I was being conned. I didn't know that Spectac's office in Holland had been asking for the original bank guarantee – to no avail.

Our bank had wanted to see it. Two days had passed and they hadn't heard from OCS.

I only became aware of the problem when I received a fax from my office. It said our bank was still having trouble locating OCS's bank in the Polynesian Islands. Although the guarantee from OCS looked fine, the bank wanted some sort of official confirmation that our money had been lodged.

When they failed to locate the bank, I was contacted and told that something was wrong.

I managed to drag O'Connor out of a meeting to ask him for some more details about this bank. I asked him why my office couldn't track down the bank manager in Polynesia.

I distinctly remember O'Connor laughing when I asked him the question.

'You know what those small islands are like,' he said. 'The manager has probably gone out fishing. Don't worry, they're never gone for more than a day or two at a time.'

He assured me that everything was in order. If I hadn't heard from the bank in Polynesia by Monday morning he'd call them himself and sort it out.

It was the 18 December. I remember thinking to myself that with a bit of luck, I'd make it home for Christmas.

Meanwhile, Hadawji called to say that there were now over 100 men screaming to get out to Thailand and work for Spectac.

So far we hadn't made a penny from OCS, and it had cost me a fortune, so I really needed to make some cash.

But I was getting worried. My bank was still trying to verify OCS's guarantee.

I told O'Connor that I was under pressure and I asked him to clear the invoice quickly to give me some breathing space.

He promised to do his best to clear both the bank guarantee and the invoice before Christmas.

With all the men now ready to go to work, there wasn't much reason for me to stay in Thailand.

I told O'Connor I was going back to Holland and that I'd be back in Thailand at the beginning of January. He promised that everything would be sorted out by then. He said he'd call the bank in Polynesia himself and find out what the hell they were playing at.

The day before I was due to leave, O'Connor called and said that one of OCS's major partners, an Arab gentleman, was in Thailand on business.

He'd seen some of Spectac's paperwork and some of the men's CVs. He said the businessman wanted to meet me before I left.

This was again all very unusual. I didn't particularly want to meet this guy, but I really didn't have much choice. You can't expect to do much business with a company if you go around refusing to have lunch with their partners. So I agreed to the meeting.

The partner pulled up at my hotel in a huge black limo. He was dressed in full Arab costume, and certainly looked the part. He was accompanied by Hayes and O'Connor, as well as a translator.

Everyone was introduced, and the translator explained that this gentleman was from Saudi Arabia. He'd been a partner and major shareholder in OCS for the last ten years or so.

Without warning, he told me that he wanted to transfer my team to a totally different project, in Saudi. OCS would understand, however, if the men wanted to go home for the holidays.

I was stunned. I had a hundred different questions running through my head, but it's difficult to argue with a man who doesn't speak any English. I sat there and listened.

When the translator had finished, I explained that it would be impossible for me to give an answer immediately.

I suggested that we stop everything, cancel the contract that already stood, then sit down and work out a completely new one. I would talk with our lawyers and, of course, the men themselves.

As the meeting drew to a close, the man handed me a gift-wrapped box. The translator explained that this was intended as a personal New Year's gift. I didn't open it but thanked him for his kindness.

I opened the box when the Arab partner left. It contained a Rolex Oyster watch, worth $3,000.

O'Connor and Hayes stayed behind to discuss the new plans. I asked about the bank guarantee and the money from the integrity bonds. I told them the contract details could wait.

O'Connor said he wasn't sure about the cash. He'd have to check with Chicago after Christmas.

I was now getting very nervous about the whole deal, but I had no option but to remain calm. I kept my composure and told O'Connor that if the men were going to go home and come back again in the New Year, they'd want their bonds returned, and rightly so. If the bonds were still required in January, they could pay them again.

O'Connor looked at me in the eye and said he was sure something could be worked out.

I left for the Philippines, where some of the men had been sent to work in the meantime.

I held a meeting and explained everything as it had been explained to me. When they heard that they were now going to work in Saudi, they were as surprised as I had been.

One of the men was wearing a suspicious expression all through the meeting. Eventually he piped up.

'This all seems very strange to me,' he said. 'A few of us have worked in Saudi before. The Saudi authorities aren't too keen on foreigners at the moment. They're trying to cut back on the number of foreign workers, not increase it.'

There were nods of agreement from around the room. I didn't have the exact details, so I couldn't clear up their doubts.

Although I remained calm, I knew something was wrong. It wasn't making sense.

I told the men that we'd get OCS to return the integrity bonds at once. Then we'd wait and see what happened after Christmas. I also planned to withdraw the money I'd lodged in the Polynesian Islands.

The men knew something was wrong. A few of them said they wanted to come back to Bangkok with me, collect their integrity bonds, then travel home for Christmas. Looking back on it now, I don't think they believed a word I was saying.

I told them to come along, by all means. But they also wanted me to pay all their air fares to Bangkok.

What no one knew was that I was broke. I'd invested every penny I had into the OCS deal. I couldn't pay their air fares. Besides, I didn't particularly want 30 men all snapping at me for action and their bond money back.

Eventually I gave them a choice. If they wanted to come to Bangkok that was okay with me, but they'd have to pay the fare themselves. I simply couldn't afford it.

Besides, I didn't suspect there was going to be any problem having the bonds returned, so I didn't think it was necessary for everyone to come with me.

But it was their choice and their money, so I didn't argue. It was now the 22 December.

I returned to Bangkok the next morning with the men. When I arrived I immediately called OCS offices.

There was no answer.

I didn't panic at first. I kept my nerve. It was almost Christmas. Offices all over the world were closed.

I had O'Connor's mobile telephone number. I dialled it, but I couldn't get through. I kept on telling myself that everything was okay. With the number of mobiles in use in Thailand that was no great surprise either.

I called Spectac's office in Holland and asked them to fax and telephone OCS in Chicago. Again, there was no answer.

It was at this stage that I began to panic.

18 of the men had returned with me to Bangkok; the others were due to arrive the next day. When they found out I hadn't been able to contact OCS, they started to panic too.

I tried to calm the men down. I explained to them that there was no reason to get alarmed just yet. I told them that once I managed to speak with O'Connor, it would all be sorted out.

The truth was that I couldn't even think straight. I continually tried to convince myself that O'Connor and OCS were legitimate. After all, someone not answering the phone wasn't enough to start making accusations of criminality and fraud.

I tried to convince myself that I was wrong and just being paranoid.

I didn't want to think I'd been so foolish as to trust a bunch of criminals. A company so businesslike and professional as OCS couldn't turn out to be thieves. Could they?

We waited and waited, but still couldn't get hold of O'Connor. There really wasn't much we could do.

Nobody wanted to involve the police. I told myself that O'Connor was probably just out of reach for a while. Not exactly a crime.

Still trying to be rational, I said we should wait, at least a little bit longer. If O'Connor was missing then our money was too, but it was probably nothing. I tried to convince myself that O'Connor had simply taken a few days off. It was Christmas, after all.

Days went by, and we still heard nothing.

Christmas came and went, and I abandoned the idea of getting home to see my family. Throughout the holiday I kept trying O'Connor's mobile and OCS's offices but still couldn't get any response from either.

I prayed and prayed. On December 27, I thought my prayers had been answered. Hadawji called to say she had received a fax from Chicago, from O'Connor.

The fax said he wished Spectac and its staff a merry Christmas. It also said that OCS hoped the New Year would be very prosperous, and that they looked forward to doing business with us.

It was all very businesslike.

I was bewildered. I clung to the hope that my gut instinct was wrong.

I told Hadawji to call Chicago and ask to speak to O'Connor. I told her to tell him to call me immediately.

She called back a few minutes later to say that when she introduced herself, O'Connor had hung up.

I didn't need to know any more. I'd been conned. O'Connor had stolen nearly half a million dollars.

3

I didn't want to believe it, but I knew I'd been taken for a fool. OCS had stolen $460,000. O'Connor had set me up. The whole deal had been an elaborate fraud. The offices, the personnel, the technical drawings. It was all a con.

I went straight to the police. They sent me to a department designated to deal with foreigners called the tourist police. I filed a complaint and was asked to come back the next morning, when an officer would be assigned my case.

Breaking the news to the men wasn't easy. As you'd expect, they were pissed off but they weren't as hostile as I'd expected them to be.

But they did blame me. They said I had got them into this mess and now I had to sort it out.

I asked some of the men to file complaints along with me, in the hope that it would be seen as a serious matter and more police would be assigned to the case. Out of the 30 men, only five agreed to make a statement. The others just sat back and expected me to take care of everything.

The following day, one of the men came with me to the police station. I also took a translator just in case there were problems with the police.

The police wanted to know every detail, from the advert in the Dutch newspaper to the final unanswered phonecall. They asked every question you could imagine. How much did my ticket cost? Where did I stay? Who did I meet? When did I pay the money? How much? Where? Where were the contracts? Where were the men?

The interrogation went on and on for hours and hours and hours. I was exhausted by the end of the day – but it was far from over.

The police ordered me to come to the station every morning. I would arrive promptly at 7.30 a.m. and they would keep me there until 6 p.m.

I couldn't stop thinking about what had happened and I blamed myself for being too anxious to make money and for taking short cuts.

To save my sanity, I started searching for the con men. It might have seemed like a futile exercise given the size of Bangkok, but it was all I could do.

After spending the entire day answering questions at the police station, I would spend another four or five hours simply going around Bangkok's bars and restaurants with photos of O'Connor and Hayes.

I had copies of their passport photographs. I also got a photo of Hayes from a barmaid who used to be his girlfriend.

I did the same thing every night. I wasn't about to give up looking. I was relentless in my pursuit.

Bangkok has thousands of motorcycle taxis, which go all over the city. I made copies of the photos and gave them to some of the motorcyclists. If they spotted O'Connor or Hayes and led me to either, I promised to pay a reward of 12,500 baht. That's a lot of money to a Thai.

The offer of a reward certainly drew a response, but it failed to locate the criminals.

After a couple of days a taxi boy came to find me. He swore on his life that he'd seen Ronnie Hayes boarding a tour bus going to Pattaya, a town located about 100 km away.

I went with him on the back of his motorcycle all the way to Pattaya. It wasn't much fun going 100 km on the back of a motorcycle without a jacket or helmet, but I couldn't afford not to.

It turned out to be a wild goose chase.

Meanwhile I contacted the tourist police every day. I gave them every shred of evidence I could find.

I handed over every piece of correspondence that I had received from OCS: the contracts, the faxes, the bank guarantee. I even gave them my own bank records.

At one point, I became a suspect. Some of the men thought I was part of the deception and the police began to check up on me.

When the men heard about this, they started to suggest amongst themselves that maybe I should be locked up, just in case.

It didn't seem to occur to any of them that if I'd wanted to steal their money I would have done it back at Schiphol Airport.

This allegation affected me more than anything. I'd been with the men every step of the way. Besides, most of the stolen money was mine. The men had lost only a few thousand each; I had lost hundreds of thousands of dollars.

The truth was that they all wanted someone to blame, and they really didn't care who it was.

The nearest Irish embassy was located in Kuala Lumpur in Malaysia. I had already contacted the Irish consulate in Bangkok but was told there was nothing that they could do.

I also got in touch with the British embassy in Bangkok. Most of the men were English, so I felt sure that at least they would get some help.

I was eventually allowed to speak with the ambassador. I explained everything that had happened in as much detail as possible. I also explained that the tourist police didn't seem to be in any hurry to get their investigation going.

But the British ambassador wasn't in a position to do anything to help us, and nor was the Irish consulate. If I was going to get my money back, I was going to have to take care of everything myself.

In the subsequent months, I sold everything that I owned. For my own watch I got 7,000 baht. For a signet ring from my mother, I managed to get 5,000 baht. Finally, I sold my wedding ring and a small gold identity bracelet for 8,000 baht.

I still had the Rolex given to me by O'Connor's bogus Arab partner. As it was brand new and still in the box, I managed to get 40,000 baht for it. When I had sold everything, I bought airline tickets for the men and sent them home.

* * *

I vowed to find O'Connor and Hayes. I was angry and wanted revenge. I went to the police every day and demanded action.

After several weeks had passed, they said they could accept my complaint and issued warrants for the arrest of O'Connor and Hayes. But there was one condition: they would take action only if I agreed to remain in Thailand.

I'd have to identify the two fraudsters after their arrest, and then give evidence in court. Without a witness, they said, it would be a waste of their time.

Not really given much choice, I said I'd stay. I took whatever work I could get as a welder and made enough money to get by.

I'd given the police the copy of O'Connor's Irish passport, complete with photo and serial number. I was told that if he left or entered Thailand, they would catch him.

Ronnie Hayes would be a little more difficult, but the police had his photo, so he wouldn't get far either.

But it didn't take me long to realise that the Thai police were corrupt and dishonest. They looked for bribes every time I met them. They were all untrustworthy and insincere.

I realised that if I was ever to get my money back I would have to find O'Connor and Hayes myself.

A month or so later, I got lucky. I was sitting outside a bar in an entertainment complex, reading a newspaper. It was about seven in the evening.

Glancing up from my paper, I noticed a man in a sharp suit, with a shock of grey hair. I couldn't believe my eyes. Strolling right in front of me was Ronnie Hayes.

Not only was it him, but he walked as though he hadn't a care in the world. He definitely wasn't in hiding, or even trying to avoid being recognised. He looked exactly the same as he had when we meet two months previously.

I felt a mixture of excitement and terror at the prospect of facing him. I watched as he disappeared into a bar. Two or three of the motorcycle taxi boys had also seen him and came running. None of us could believe we had found him.

Not wanting to miss the chance, I walked into the bar and pulled up a stool beside him. When he saw me, his mouth dropped open.

'Hello, Ronnie,' I said. 'I believe you have something that belongs to me.'

He regained his composure hastily, and made an effort to remain nonchalant.

'I don't know what you're talking about,' he said.

I smashed him with a head butt.

I hit him again a few times, but the motorcycle boys pulled me away. It didn't matter anyway; I had him and he wasn't going anywhere.

I asked the barman to call the tourist police, and gave him the mobile number for the lieutenant in charge of my case.

The police arrived minutes later and Hayes stumbled out to their pick-up. The lieutenant told me that I shouldn't have hit him.

I asked him what was I supposed to do? I told him that I wasn't about to give him a chance either to fight or to run.

To be honest, it felt good to thump the bastard. He'd caused me a lot of pain. In that moment, I didn't really care about the consequences of my actions, and I certainly hadn't been thinking about the law.

Hayes tried to bluff his way out of custody. He said he thought O'Connor and OCS were genuine. He actually said he had nothing to do with the financial dealings of OCS and claimed that he was a victim too.

He said he'd quit working for OCS in December because they hadn't paid him.

I didn't believe a word of it. I told him that the police had already rounded up all the secretaries and office staff he and O'Connor had hired. I was lying through my teeth, but he didn't know that.

Eventually I proposed a deal. If he returned his share of the money they'd stolen, and if he was willing to help the police to find O'Connor, then I would talk to his trial judge and say that he was only a small player in the scam.

I knew O'Connor was the boss. I wanted him more than Hayes.

It didn't take Hayes long to betray his partner. Criminals are all the same. They'll always sell each other out. He claimed that O'Connor had only paid him $80,000, of which he had spent some on a holiday, but that he still had $60,000 left – about 1.5 million baht.

Pleading for mercy, he said he would hand over all of it if I promised to keep to our agreement. I said I would.

The police agreed to the proposition and offered to take Hayes to the bank to withdraw the money. I said I would return the next day to collect the cash. I decided to bring a lawyer with me, just to make sure that everything was legal and above board.

This turned out to be a good idea.

When we got to the police station the next morning, Hayes had changed his mind. When he withdrew my 1.5 million baht from his account, the police had apparently seen their opportunity, and began to give him all sorts of advice. They actually told him that he didn't have to return the money until after the court case.

They advised him to charge me with assault. And they also encouraged him to demand that I drop all charges against him before returning the stolen money.

I now found myself on the losing side once again – but there was no way I was going to drop the charges. I asked the lawyer for his advice.

Speaking with brutal honesty, my lawyer said I didn't have a choice. If I didn't drop the charges and take the money, then Hayes would use it to make bail, and get out anyway. If I wanted the money back, I was going to have to accept the deal.

Against my better judgement, I took the money and dropped the charges.

Nothing is what it seems in Bangkok. When it came to counting the money before signing for it, it was short. There was a lot missing – a little from each stack of bills, but totalling around 100,000 baht (US $400). The police had helped themselves.

There were two policemen in the room where I counted the money. They kept staring at me. I asked the lawyer what to do. He whispered that it would be best just to finish counting, take the money, and go. If we complained that there was money missing, it would mean the police would have to have an internal investigation, and they'd hold the money for longer.

It had only been in the police station overnight and there was 100,000 baht missing. I wondered how much would be missing by the end of the investigation.

After I finished counting the cash, I withdrew my complaint against Hayes. He had been using this pseudonymn for years, I found out, and was from New Zealand – not Australia. This was the reason, the police said, they hadn't been able to find him.

Before finally withdrawing the charge, I made it clear to Hayes that any one of the 30 men could re-charge him at any time. I wanted him to know that he wasn't home free. He was going to have to help find O'Connor whether he liked it or not.

This frightened him to the extent that he suddenly remembered where O'Connor lived, and where his favourite restaurants and bars were.

Thinking that they were going to earn more money, the investigation team offered to drive to O'Connor's house and arrest him.

Hayes said O'Connor lived about 30 km away.

I waited in the patrol car while the officers went into the apartment. After about half an hour, they came back. They said O'Connor wasn't there and had checked out.

But they said they would now place a spy there. They promised that if O'Connor ever returned to his apartment they would get him. He wouldn't escape.

There wasn't much more I could do.

I took some solace when I read the morning papers the next day. When I first started searching for O'Connor and Hayes, I contacted a number of journalists who highlighted my case. They had reported the original con and now they reported about how I had caught Hayes.

This prompted Hayes to leave Thailand the moment he was released from custody. His cover blown, he jetted off to destinations unknown.

Now the only thing left for me to do was wait for news of O'Connor.

There wasn't any point in going back to Europe anyway. I had lost everything. The bank had taken my business and repossessed my house to pay back the money I'd borrowed. My wife had left me and taken our three children back to Ireland. I had nothing left but time on my hands.

4

In time, I built a new life for myself in Thailand. I gradually got used to Bangkok, its climate and its food. You could say that I gradually immersed myself into the city's culture.

I grew to love the smells and sounds of the city, its people and even the constant traffic.

I also got to know my way around the city and its back streets. I moved into a small house outside the city. I bought food in the local market every week and discovered the joys of eating Thai food. I enjoyed a good quality of life.

All the time, the people fascinated me. While warm and friendly, they looked upon all foreigners as outsiders or as a potential means to escaping whatever problems they had. I would in time learn that nothing they said could be taken at face value, but at that time I was alone.

And I was desperately lonely.

I missed my children who lived with their mother in Ireland. I would talk to them by phone but I often felt like there was a part of me missing.

They say every cloud has a silver lining. I thought that mine was Nanglung, a beautiful-looking girl who had acted as my translator during my dealings with O'Connor and Hayes.

Nanglung and I had remained friends after O'Connor vanished. Her name meant Waterfall and I found her exotic and alluring. When I decided to stay in Thailand and search for O'Connor, she helped me. I was wild about her. I couldn't help but fall for her. Everything about her was beautiful.

Don't get me wrong – I'd be the first one to put my hands up and say that I don't think she loved me for my looks or in any genuine way.

Thai women become involved with European men for various reasons. Some give themselves over for genuine love, but others do it for money.

Nanglung was mostly interested in me because she believed I had money. I was attracted to her for all the obvious reasons, though I have to say it wasn't the same as dating a girl back home. I knew the foundations that our relationship was built on. But you must remember that I was alone and far away from home.

Eventually we got married. But when I say married, I don't mean it in the conventional sense.

After we lived together for some time, she brought me home to meet her parents. Nanglung grew up on a farm in the provinces outside the city.

I remember arriving at her village which was rural and backward. Her parents lived in a small house and could not understand a word of English, but I could tell they were delighted she was marrying a foreigner. It was all very surreal.

At the time, there were two separate types of marriage in Thailand. The first was a Buddhist ceremony of traditional Thai marriage, and the other was a legal process of marriage registration with the Thai authorities.

Nanglung chose to marry me in a Buddhist ceremony which simply involved me visiting her village and asking her parents for her hand in marriage. I had no interest in entering into a legal marriage because I was still married.

The traditional arrangement suited me fine. In Thailand, a couple gets engaged during a ceremony known as *Thong Mun*. This involved me giving gold to Nanglung.

Whether traditional or official, Thai marriages involve a tradition called *Sinsod*. This is the custom of paying a dowry to compensate the bride's family for the mother's milk. Although I was told there was no set amount, the sum was determined by the suitor's wealth. In my case, her family believed the *Farang*, or foreigner, marrying their daughter was wealthy. Little did they know. I gave them some money and they seemed genuinely delighted. The whole village shook my hand that day.

I have to say that the whole experience didn't mean that much to me. I couldn't talk to her parents or hold a conversation with her family, but I was obviously being taken quite seriously by everyone concerned. Her parents certainly regarded our wedding as a lifelong commitment. In the eyes of the Buddhist religion, marriage is sacred and everlasting.

I did love Nanglung. She was my only real friend at the time. At the time, I would have done anything for her. In fact, I did everything, and more and she reciprocated it. She fell pregnant soon after we moved in together. Almost a year later, she gave birth to a son. I called him Brendan.

* * *

Although I now lived in domestic harmony, I never stopped searching for O'Connor. He became my obsession. I checked his favourite bars and restaurants regularly and I continued to pay the motorcycle taxi boys to look out for him.

I also kept in contact with the police, and telephoned them at least once a month to check on the progress of the investigation.

The answer I received was always the same: they were still looking for O'Connor, but they said he hadn't left or entered Thailand, or even returned to his apartment since the fraud.

I didn't trust them one bit and continued to offer a reward for any information on his whereabouts. This generated some leads from time to time. I'd rush off to a bar or a restaurant after getting a tip-off to say he was there, but it would never be him.

One time, a friend of mine came back from a holiday in the Philippines and swore that he'd spotted O'Connor. I caught a flight the next day to Manila. I found the town, I found the bar, I even found a prostitute O'Connor had spent the previous night with. She showed me his hotel, but he had already checked out. He had vanished once again.

Still, I didn't give up.

Two and a half years passed before I got a real lead. And it happened in the most unlikely of places. Because I was European, I was forced to leave Thailand every three months in order to get a new tourist visa.

I often travelled into countries neighbouring Thailand for a few hours or a day to give the impression that I was a tourist travelling through the region. On one such trip in June 1997, I crossed the border into Laos to spend a few hours shopping before returning to Thailand.

While I was in Laos I met an Australian man, and we got talking. One thing led to another, and I told him my story.

After I'd finished, he said that he knew a man who fitted O'Connor's description. At the time, I carried a picture of O'Connor with me at all times, and I showed this to him.

'That's him,' he said. 'That's Mitch!'

Mitch, he told me, was a crook – a professional con artist – and was best known for selling and dealing in fake diamonds. He had organised scams selling fictitious gold and diamond mines, and even sold fake share certificates. To the best of my friend's knowledge, at the moment he was involved in something to do with construction machinery.

He said he didn't have Mitch's address or phone number, but would try his best to locate him for me. I gave him my work and home phone numbers.

A few weeks passed without any news. Then when I went home one night, my wife told me that someone had called and wanted me to call them as soon as possible. It was my friend.

He told me that O'Connor was currently operating a construction scam in Bangkok. He gave me his address and phone number. This was the closest I'd ever got to O'Connor.

I was determined to make no mistakes. If living in Bangkok had taught me one thing, it was not to trust the police.

So I decided to find O'Connor myself. I planned to entrap him and call in the police when I had him cornered.

I felt alive for the first time in years. I quickly began investigating O'Connor – and discovered that he had never even moved out of his apartment.

I hadn't bothered checking his apartment because I didn't think anybody would be stupid enough to stay at the same address if they knew the police were out looking for them.

It was then that I realised that the police had been lying to me for years. They'd never looked for O'Connor, and they'd certainly never tried to arrest him.

There was only one explanation that made sense: O'Connor must have paid them off. Nobody could walk around so freely if the police were really trying to arrest them. Nothing else made sense.

Given that I knew I couldn't trust them, I figured there was a good chance that they'd tip him off if I told them of my plan.

I tried to remain calm.

I knew I couldn't risk phoning him, just in case he recognised my voice. So I asked one of the secretaries at the company I was working for at the time to do it for me. She phoned O'Connor and explained that she worked for a large construction company, and her boss had heard he had some machinery for sale. She said the boss was interested in buying equipment if the price was right.

O'Connor took the bait. When I arrived at work the next morning, I found a fax waiting for me. It was signed Mitch. He'd sent an introduction letter and a list of his machinery for sale and the price per machine.

I couldn't believe it – his company was called Offshore Construction Services. He hadn't even bothered to think up a new name.

Although I wanted to go and punch his lights out there and then, I knew I had to play the long game. If I jumped straight in he'd know something was wrong.

So I responded to his fax in writing and asked for more information about the machinery for sale. I signed off as Mr Bill Turner.

For the first time in years, I felt as if I was winning. I asked a number of friends for help.

An American friend of mine called Chuck offered to play the role of Bill Turner.

Chuck telephoned O'Connor and told him that he was interested in some of his machinery, and arranged to meet at our offices to discuss prices and payment.

I told Chuck to offer O'Connor an incentive to arrive on time. He told O'Connor that if they could reach an agreement at the meeting, then he would place a cash deposit on the machinery. Chuck offered him $300,000 up front.

O'Connor said he'd be there.

I knew we had him. The cash deposit would bring him for sure. He wouldn't trust anybody else with that amount of cash and would come himself. But I still had a hell of a lot to do before the meeting.

A friend of mine had a brother in the police. I asked him and another officer to attend the meeting and arrest O'Connor when he arrived.

I explained everything to them in detail, and why I couldn't trust the tourist police in Bangkok. They both agreed to help.

Now I only needed somewhere to hold the meeting.

The solution turned out to be easy. The company I was working for was in the middle of building a new construction yard and offices. Most of the buildings were half finished, but there was a small office block that had just been completed. It would be perfect.

I faxed O'Connor a map giving directions to the office and set the date of the meeting for 21 July 1997, at 1 p.m.

Everything went according to plan. But I was still worried that O'Connor might not come alone. If he brought a lot of men with him, I would be in trouble. So I asked my secretary to ask for the names of those who would be attending the meeting, and some form of photo ID so that our security people could issue them with passes.

O'Connor didn't suspect a thing, and faxed a copy of his passport immediately. He also sent one belonging to a man named Brett Holdsworth.

He was O'Connor's bodyguard. Would you believe that O'Connor actually said that Holdsworth was coming in case we gave him a large amount of cash? He really thought that we'd fallen for his con and he was coming to pick up an easy $300,000.

On the morning of 21 July, everything was going according to plan. I had set up the office with a clear view of the main gate to see O'Connor when he arrived.

We waited for little under 30 minutes before O'Connor arrived. Chuck greeted him, then escorted him to the office.

I can vividly recall Chuck approaching O'Connor with his hand outstretched. After they shook hands, Chuck pointed O'Connor and Holdsworth in our direction and asked O'Connor to wait inside, before making an excuse and disappearing.

Next, one of my Thai friends went to the door and ushered O'Connor and Holdsworth in. I was sitting behind a desk in the office, with two armed police positioned just behind the door.

O'Connor came in first, followed by his bodyguard. When he saw me, he stopped dead. All he could say was, 'It's you!'

O'Connor next looked at the police, then back at me. He was trapped and he knew it.

Then he rushed at me.

All hell broke lose. He threw a few punches at me, then I managed to grab his arm and he wrestled me to the floor. Holdsworth stepped in, but one of the policemen immediately put a hand on his shoulder. He backed off, noticing that the policeman's other hand was on his holster.

I belted O'Connor in the face. I wanted to kill him there and then. The bastard had destroyed my life.

The police had to pry us apart. O'Connor was built like a prop forward and far too strong for me, but I didn't care. I locked on to him and continued to punch him in the face.

When I finally stopped hitting him, I noticed that I'd left a slight mark under his left eye, but apart from that he wasn't hurt.

He was bloody angry though. I don't know if it was because he'd been caught by one of his own scams, or if it was simply because he'd been caught, but he was not a happy man. His eyes kept darting around the room and his face was purple with rage.

The police now spoke and told O'Connor to sit down. Once he was sitting he seemed to recover himself slightly.

'What the hell is going on?' he barked. 'I am a businessman. I did not come to this office to be attacked!'

My police friends told O'Connor that I had made a complaint against him, and then explained what I'd told them. O'Connor said that he didn't know me and had never seen me before in his life.

This was all bullshit and everybody knew it. So the police laid it out very simply. He could either admit that he stole the money, or he could go to prison.

O'Connor thought about this for a minute.

'Wait! Wait a minute,' he said. 'Maybe I do remember doing some business with Mr Martin. I didn't steal any money, but Mr Martin might have lost out on the deal. I'm sure we can come to some agreement. Perhaps we could talk in private,' he added, looking at me.

I still remember the look on his face. It struck me for the first time that O'Connor looked on fraud and deception just like any other business. Everything was a matter of negotiation.

'No chance, O'Connor,' I said. 'If you want to say something, you can say it here, in front of the police.'

I asked the police to take him away. The police stepped in and started to cuff him — at which point my wife appeared, with four of her brothers. She had been worried that something had gone wrong, or that O'Connor's bodyguard had come to the meeting armed.

In fact, for a bodyguard, Holdsworth had been very well behaved. He'd sat quietly against the wall and hadn't interfered.

Nevertheless, Nanglung's arrival with her four brothers made me feel a bit more relaxed. You can never trust a Thai cop 100 per cent, especially if there's money involved.

I told O'Connor there was no deal. He could either return the money or go to prison. To be honest, I would have preferred if he had opted to go to prison.

For the first time, O'Connor looked worried. He said he'd give me three million baht. He'd stolen about 20 million. I told him to fuck off and not to insult me.

He then offered to pay me 11 million baht, saying this was every penny he had. Allowing for what he would have had to spend on the con itself and paying off his partners, I figured he was telling the truth.

Not wanting to sound desperate, I told him that I'd consider dropping the charges but only after he'd returned the money. Of course, I had no intention of dropping the charges, but I knew that if O'Connor ended up in any police station with pockets full of cash, he would bribe his way to freedom.

Acting all friendly, he said that I'd have to take him to his bank in Bangkok if I wanted to collect the money myself. No local bank would hand out 11 million baht.

That left me with a problem. I knew the police couldn't take O'Connor to Bangkok unless they arrested him. As a warrant was supposed to have been issued in Bangkok for O'Connor's arrest, their superiors would have to notify the tourist police, and O'Connor would to end up in their hands.

That was the last thing I needed. After three years of lies and bullshit I knew I couldn't trust the tourist police – and if O'Connor had paid them once he would do it again. I'd have to bring O'Connor to Bangkok myself.

* * *

The plan ran into difficulties from the beginning. The bodyguard, Holdsworth, was the biggest problem. I should have refused to allow him to attend the meeting in the first place.

Now he was putting me in a difficult position. If I let Holdsworth go, he might phone Bangkok and arrange some unpleasant surprises for me. Or he might call the police.

I'd have to bring him along. But I reckoned that with my wife's four brothers accompanying me, I would see no trouble out of him.

This was my biggest mistake.

I paid the policemen for their time and they left, saying that if there was any trouble I could call them.

O'Connor had arrived to the meeting in an old American-style car with a full front seat.

I got into the driver's seat, and sandwiched O'Connor between me and one of my companions. Holdsworth sat in the back.

My wife Nanglung travelled in a pick-up truck driven by one of her brothers.

The first stop was home. We had to drop Nanglung off to take care of my son. The drive home took a few hours.

We arrived at my house at 4 p.m. which meant it was too late to drive to Bangkok city. I would have to wait until the morning to withdraw the cash.

There wasn't much point in everyone sitting outside my house in cars, so I invited O'Connor and Holdsworth inside until I could figure out what to do.

In truth, I was falling to pieces. I couldn't think straight. I knew there was no way I could keep O'Connor and Holdsworth in my home until the next day.

Knowing my luck, he would have me charged with false imprisonment or kidnapping.

My wife gave me, O'Connor and Holdsworth a beer each and we began chatting awkwardly. I took the opportunity to ask O'Connor why he had stolen so much money.

'Why didn't you just take the contracts? You'd still have made a lot of money.'

O'Connor just shrugged his shoulders.

'Surely to God you knew that for almost half a million dollars somebody would come looking for you?' I continued.

'Why?' said O'Connor. 'Nobody's ever come looking for me before.'

He was completely shameless. He just didn't care.

He explained that I'd given him and his 'team' endless headaches. He said they'd had to put a lot of extra work into the fraud. He said that I was a real professional and obviously knew my stuff.

He then caught me off guard. What he said next really bowled me over. He actually asked me to join him as a partner.

'Think about it,' he said, smiling. 'There's a lot of money to be made.'

I could feel an immense inner rage well up inside my body. I wanted to smash his head in with my fists.

O'Connor had ruined my life. I'd lost my business, my house, my wife Paula and my children – not to mention the $460,000. And here was this bastard asking me if I'd like to do the same to other people.

He knew by the way I was looking at him that I wanted to attack him there and then.

I couldn't listen to his bullshit, so I stood up and walked outside to speak with my wife's three brothers who were waiting outside on the porch. The youngest brother waited inside with O'Connor and Holdsworth.

I discussed everything with them and we decided that we would go to Bangkok later that night. I didn't want them near my wife and my baby boy.

Instead, we'd wait at O'Connor's house until the bank opened in the morning. Then I'd go with O'Connor, collect the money, give it to my lawyer in Bangkok, then hand O'Connor over to the police. Without the money O'Connor wouldn't be able to pay them off.

It seemed like a good plan – and anyway, it was the best that any of us could come up with.

I went back into the house and told O'Connor and Holdsworth that we were leaving for Bangkok in a couple of hours.

I wasn't about to ask Nanglung to cook for these bastards, so I told them, 'If you want to eat, give me the money and I'll send someone out for it. You can pay for it yourselves. And another thing. I want money for petrol. I'm not going to fork out to take you scumbags to Bangkok.'

Actually, I wanted to see how much cash O'Connor was carrying. I didn't want to give him the chance to bribe anybody.

Nanglung was deeply worried about the whole plan and wanted to drive with us, but I didn't think that was a good idea.

This trip wasn't exactly a family outing. And although I was terrified, I told her that I'd be all right and not to worry.

At that time, I couldn't speak any Thai, so I asked Nanglung to explain again to her brothers what they had to do. She told them to drive to Bangkok and make sure I wasn't attacked.

We took O'Connor's car because it was bigger and more comfortable.

During the journey, the bodyguard found his voice. Up until then, he hadn't spoken a word.

'I would really think about going into business with Mitch if I were you,' he said. 'He knows what he's doing. Come on, if he could con you he must be good! Together you'd make millions.'

Holdsworth was really getting on my nerves. I didn't want to dignify this shit with an argument, so I told him to shut the fuck up.

O'Connor and Holdsworth next started asking if we could stop for a piss. It was about another hour's drive to Bangkok, so I said I'd stop at the first service station. But after another ten minutes they started complaining again.

Some of the brothers mumbled something about needing to go too, so I pulled over onto the hard shoulder.

Everyone got out and relieved themselves. My wife's brothers got back into the car and nodded off to sleep, which is typical of Thai people. If they sit still for five minutes, they're asleep. This gave O'Connor and Holdsworth the opportunity they were waiting for – to attack me and try to escape.

I can still recall parts of what happened.

I remember O'Connor leaning against the open front passenger-side door to my right while Holdsworth was on my left.

Once I was alone, O'Connor shouted, 'Now!'

Holdsworth spun around and came at me. He had a knife.

I took a quick look at O'Connor, then turned to face the bodyguard. He took a step towards me and slashed at me with his blade. When his arm came out for the swing I stepped in.

I hit him as hard as I could. I knew that I wouldn't get a second chance; if he brought the knife down I was dead.

I reached for his arm with my left hand and belted him in the stomach with my right fist. Then I got him with a head-butt. We rolled down the steep embankment at the edge of the road.

Holdsworth grabbed me by the throat as I was trying to get up, so I punched him in the nuts.

He was still landing blows on me – so I hit him, and kept on hitting him until he stopped.

I thought he was going to kill me. I believed I was going to die.

When he came at me again, I hit him with every ounce of power I had left. When he fell, he pulled me with him. We both crashed to the ground, and it was over. I'd knocked Holdsworth out.

I fumbled around in the darkness and managed to scramble to my feet. I cursed the ground that Holdsworth walked on, and made my way back to the car.

5

The brothers awoke upon hearing the commotion, and one of them climbed down the embankment to help me up. When I climbed back up to the car, O'Connor was smiling.

'You're a tough little bastard, aren't you?' he said.

I would have loved to have gone over to him and knocked that bloody smirk off his face, but I just didn't have the energy.

My body hurt. I was scratched and bruised all over. My mouth was cut, and my nose was bleeding. There were gashes under and over my left eye, and a slash wound on my left arm. My shirt was ripped and cut to ribbons.

I looked back down the embankment to see where Holdsworth was. But now there was no sign of him. I asked O'Connor what he wanted to do about his friend.

There was a spotlight in his car that connected to the cigarette lighter. He plugged it in and shone it down the embankment.

But we couldn't find him. We flashed the light back and forth for about ten minutes, but we still couldn't see him.

'Useless bastard,' said O'Connor. 'He's probably run off to hide in the woods somewhere. Leave him. He'll be all right.'

I didn't care. I wasn't going to sit there and wait for him to come at me again.

Everybody got back into the car and we drove on to O'Connor's house in Bangkok without any further problems. O'Connor was quiet most of the way.

We parked and went up to the one-bedroom apartment that O'Connor shared with his Thai wife. His wife didn't seem concerned that he had arrived home with five other men.

I asked if I could go and wash up because I'd had an 'accident'. I didn't mention the fight with the bodyguard, and she didn't ask.

I washed my face and hands, and the cuts and bruises, then went back to sit down. O'Connor's wife brought me a beer and gave O'Connor a large whisky.

The Thai boys said they didn't want a drink, but would go and get something to eat. I didn't object. They hadn't provided much protection so far.

Anyway, I didn't think O'Connor would try any bullshit – not in his own house. The neighbours would call the police if he did.

With the brothers gone, O'Connor sat down opposite me at the table. He handed me three cheques.

Two were in sterling for a total of about £16,000, which he said were from a legitimate business deal. The last one was in the name of Brett Holdsworth, and was for a total of about one million New Zealand dollars.

This, he explained, was O'Connor's payment for making Holdsworth a full partner. Apparently the bodyguard wasn't happy with being only a bodyguard. He wanted part of the action.

O'Connor said I could hold the cheques as a sign of good faith until we went to the bank in the morning. I took the cheques but didn't have much faith in any of them getting cashed.

After a while he asked me if I would like to get a hotel for the night and come back for him in the morning. What a bastard. He honestly thought that I would drop my knickers and let him fuck me again. It had taken me three years to catch him. I wasn't about to leave and come back in the morning to an empty house.

I told him that I was a big boy. I would sleep on the floor in front of the door. O'Connor's apartment was on the fourth floor and the balcony was all fenced in with an iron grate. I knew he couldn't jump out even if he wanted to.

There'd been no arguing or fighting since we'd arrived at O'Connor's place. Both he and his wife had been polite, even friendly, so when his wife said that she would go and buy some food rather than cook herself, I didn't protest.

She wasn't a hostage, and she really had nothing to do with my problems. Besides, I didn't think she was fully aware of what was going on.

We didn't have much more to say to each other. The two of us sat there and watched a video. I was glad to have something to take my mind off the situation.

O'Connor's wife had been gone 20 minutes when I heard a knock on the door. I thought it was Nanglung's four brothers. Or maybe O'Connor's wife had forgotten her key. As I was sitting near the door I got up to answer it.

It was the police.

As I opened the door I stepped back a little into the room. The first police officer moved in quickly and punched me straight in the mouth. Two others came in behind him and grabbed me so I couldn't move.

O'Connor was shouting, 'That's him, that's him!' and pointing at me. 'Watch him, he's dangerous!' he yelled. 'He's one of the Irish IRA!'

Another police officer came in with O'Connor's wife. He spoke good English and asked me what was going on.

Apparently, after the wife had left the apartment, she'd called the police and said that I was threatening O'Connor and trespassing in their apartment.

I calmly explained everything that had happened, including the fact that an arrest warrant had been issued for O'Connor already for stealing the $460,000 – or at least, I hoped it had.

The police listened, then walked over to O'Connor and handcuffed him. They apologised for the misunderstanding, but said I'd still need to go with them to the police station to identify the fraudster officially. O'Connor was led away kicking and screaming, protesting his innocence.

* * *

Unfortunately, as the original complaint had been made to the tourist police, and because O'Connor was a foreigner, everything was handed over to them. And that was where my real troubles began.

We waited at the police station for some time. Eventually, O'Connor was led away and I was taken into the captain's office. It was the same officer I'd made the original complaint to three years ago. When he saw me he just smiled, smugly.

I was glad I had a chance to confront him.

'Why didn't you arrest O'Connor?' I asked. 'He never left Thailand. He was living in the same house, driving the same car, even using the same God damn telephone number!'

His answer was simple.

'Why didn't you pay me?' he said. 'If you'd paid me I would have arrested him.'

I could have argued that it was actually his job to arrest criminals, but I didn't think there was much point. He was corrupt, just like the rest of them.

I explained everything over and over again, in the smallest of detail. The interrogation went on and on for hours. But there were a few things I kept from them.

I didn't tell them who Chuck really was, because I'd promised not to involve him if possible. The Aussie expat who'd given me O'Connor's number also wanted his part kept quiet, so I said that I'd just phoned O'Connor's house on the spur of the moment. It was a lie, but only a white lie. I kept my word, and that was more important.

Once the police captain was satisfied that he knew everything, he reached over to his fridge and took out two tins of beer. As we drank, he congratulated me on catching O'Connor and for being so clever as to trap him with his own trick.

He asked me to wait at the tourist police office to make a preliminary identification. He said his officers were checking their files for any other complaints against O'Connor, Mitch or the boss of OCS. I knew him in all three guises, so if a charge came up under any of his names I could identify him.

In the meantime, I went out and had something to eat in the restaurant next door. I sensed no problems.

I thought they would charge O'Connor with fraud or theft, or force him to repay the money in order to get some cash from me. I phoned Nanglung and told her I wouldn't be home for another few hours.

When I went back into the tourist police, O'Connor had been brought back from the cells and was being questioned. I'd given the police O'Connor's cheques. He was busy explaining to the police where he'd got them.

When it came to the last cheque, he said, 'This is from my partner, Mr Brett Holdsworth.' Then he turned, pointed at me, and added, 'And he killed him!'

Everyone in the room looked at me.

I knew that O'Connor would try to worm his way out of it any way that he could, but I hadn't expected him to accuse me of murder.

'What the fuck is he talking about?' was the first thing out of my mouth.

I'd already told the police that Holdsworth had attacked me, that we'd had a fight and that he'd run off somewhere. I explained that Holdsworth wasn't O'Connor's partner, he was his bodyguard. Nobody was dead, or even hurt – although they had tried to kill me. There had been no murder. O'Connor was lying.

But he insisted.

'He killed my partner,' he said. 'And I can prove it. I'll show you where he's hidden the body, if one of his gang hasn't already moved it.'

O'Connor explained that I'd kidnapped him and his partner while he was at a business meeting with a man named Bill Turner. He said that I'd demanded ten million baht, and when he'd refused to pay, I'd killed his partner and then forced him to take me to his apartment, where I'd stolen the three cheques.

He then claimed that I'd held him and his wife hostage until he could take me to his bank in the morning. He said he wasn't a criminal – he was a businessman.

I tried to interrupt a few times but the police told me to be quiet and let him finish. They listened attentively to him.

It was at this point that I began to worry and fear for my own safety.

The police asked him how I'd killed his partner.

'He beat him up, then gutted him like a fish,' said O'Connor.

The police next asked him where the body was.

'His gang dragged the body off into the woods,' he said. 'If you give me a road map, I'll show you.'

A road map was found, and O'Connor pointed to a spot on it.

'That's where he did him,' he said.

I didn't pay much attention to where O'Connor had pointed. I just thought he was playing some kind of game. The police next asked me where I'd stopped the car, but I didn't know.

They asked could it have been the same place that O'Connor had pointed to?

I told them that I didn't know that either. How would I? I had simply pulled over for a piss. I didn't mark it on a map.

They were now suspicious. I could tell from their body language that they certainly didn't believe me. And the more worked up I became, the more their suspicions were aroused. I tried to calm down.

Eventually the captain said that they'd have to check out his story. After all, murder is a serious charge.

I had no problem with that. If the police wanted to waste their time that was fine by me.

I was taken back into the police captain's office, where he told me if there was anything I wanted to tell him, now would be a good time.

I told him I had no idea what O'Connor was playing at. Yes, I did fight with Holdsworth, but I hadn't killed anybody. In fact, he'd tried to kill me! I still considered myself lucky he hadn't succeeded.

The captain said he'd leave me alone to think about it. So I thought.

Why would O'Connor come out with such a story? The only reason that I could think of was that he was trying to take me to prison with him.

We'd go back to where the fight had been. All the signs of a struggle would be there, maybe even some blood. We'd fought beside the road, tumbled down the embankment and then we'd thrashed it out down in the long grass. It would be difficult to prove I was the intended victim.

And Holdsworth was missing. I didn't know where he lived or anything about him. If I couldn't find Holdsworth, I couldn't prove he was alive.

The police would hold me on suspicion of murder until they could find Holdsworth, which could be months or even years.

So O'Connor wasn't so stupid after all. He'd be an eye-witness to the alleged murder of his partner. Without Holdsworth turning up I couldn't prove O'Connor was lying. I'd go to prison until they investigated it.

Nothing made sense to me. The police were now interrogating me about Holdsworth's murder.

The situation was turning into a living nightmare. I was consumed by a dreadful feeling. I sensed that there was going to be serious trouble ahead.

At around 2 p.m. the police captain came back and told me that they'd take us back to where the fight had occurred, and then back to the construction yard where we'd held the meeting.

'Don't worry,' he said with a smirk. 'Today you go free – or you go to the monkey house with your friend.'

I didn't find it very funny. I was now beginning to panic.

I was taken out to the police minibus, and handcuffed.

We headed off towards Chonburi, the district where the fight had occurred. We made very slow progress because the traffic around the city was very heavy, and after going about 50 km the captain said that we were turning back.

When we'd arrived back at the police station, O'Connor was taken back to the cells. I was taken upstairs into the station. I asked the captain to remove the handcuffs.

'Just a moment,' he said. 'When we get to the office, I take them off.'

There was something menacing about his body language. I knew something was wrong.

6

The captain directed me towards an empty office. When I came to the office door, he pushed me through it. I landed in the middle of the room and the door was closed behind me. There was no light. I was terrified.

The door opened again. Suddenly, six or seven men rushed in, and immediately started kicking the shit out of me.

They never said a word: they just beat and kicked me. I couldn't defend myself because I was handcuffed. I just curled up on the floor and waited for it to end. I had no other choice. It was brutal.

After a couple of minutes they left as quickly as they'd come.

I just lay on the floor, bewildered. What the fuck was going on?

After about 20 minutes the light snapped on. I moved myself back into a corner and prepared for a second attack.

The door opened, and I braced myself.

The police captain walked in with two other officers. He never said a word; he just stared at me. The three men came over to me in the corner. I was still squinting from the light coming on suddenly, but I could just about make out their features. They stood over me and gave me a couple of hard kicks, then asked, 'Why did you kill your friend?'

'Fuck off!' I yelled. 'I haven't killed anybody! What the fuck is going on?'

The only answer I got was, 'Confess now, or you'll be sorry!'

'Confess to what?' I screamed. 'I haven't done anything! But if you take off these handcuffs, I'll rip your fucking head off!'

I threatened them because I was panicking. I had heard stories and rumours about police brutality. All I could think about was getting out. At that moment I didn't care about the money. I just wanted to escape.

All I remember about that moment was images of my life flashing before me. I thought they were going to kill me. I was trapped; my nerves went and I desperately tried to imagine ways of escaping.

After subjecting me to more brutality, the three police left, closed the door, and a few seconds afterwards, turned out the light again. I tried my best to remain calm but I couldn't.

After what seemed like an hour or so, they came back. The light snapped on again and this time five officers came.

There was a table and some chairs in another corner of the room, which I hadn't noticed before. One of the officers brought over a chair, dragged me to my feet, then pushed me down onto it.

One officer stood behind me, holding my shoulders down, and there was one on either side of me holding down an arm and a leg each. Another one picked up two big telephone directories and stood to my right, just out of my line of vision.

The fifth officer picked up another chair and came and sat in front of me. They never said a word to me or even spoke to each other.

I felt like getting sick. I knew they were going to torture me but I couldn't believe it was going to happen. I found this sensation terrifying. I pleaded with them to let me go but they wouldn't. I begged one of them to help me. My breathing became deeper and deeper as I tried to relax and prepare myself for pain.

Suddenly the officer sitting on the chair nodded at the officer to my right.

Immediately, my head went numb.

The policeman had smashed two telephone directories against my skull. The pain went straight to the base of my spine. It was excruciating.

'Why did you kill your friend?' he barked. Droplets of spit landed on my eyes and face.

'I don't know what you're talking about!' I screamed.

He struck me again.

'We know you killed him!'

'I didn't kill anybody!'

They attacked me in this way again and again. I tried to cope as best I could. I tried not to break down, but I couldn't hold myself together.

Telephone directories are heavy and when someone brings one down hard on your skull, it hurts, believe me. After they've done it ten times you're seeing stars. They don't leave any marks, but they cause unbelievable pain.

I was sure that shocking my brain every time with heavy blows would lead to severe damage. I imagined myself sustaining a serious brain injury.

After about 20 minutes, the beating stopped. The officers got up abruptly and left, and the light went out again.

My nose had started to bleed. I could feel the blood trickling down my lip and taste it in my mouth. My head throbbed. I was in pain.

I felt excruciating pain in my neck and shoulders. If I'd received another couple of whacks with those phone books, I'd have passed out.

After another hour or so, they came back again. When they switched the light on this time, six or seven cops stampeded through the door.

I hadn't moved, and when they came charging in they knocked me flying out of the chair. I struggled to get up but with my hands cuffed it was difficult.

The police captain stood in front of me and the others circled around. He never said a word. None of them spoke; they just stared at me. Then the captain nodded, and the others grabbed me.

I was terrified. I screamed at them for mercy.

This time, they had small circles cut out of cloth. They held me down and placed the cloth over my eyes and put a blindfold on. They already had me in handcuffs, but now they also tied my hands with cloth. Everything was prepared and they knew exactly what they were doing. They had obviously done this before.

I screamed for help. I prayed for someone to come and stop them. I would have given anything. I begged them to listen. I couldn't stop crying but they never hesitated once. My pleas for mercy went unheeded.

They sat me cross-legged on the floor. I could tell by the direction of the voices that one cop stood behind me, one on either side, and the captain stood in front with two more.

They then all let go of their grip. I didn't dare hope they had decided to stop torturing me, but I wasn't sure what was happening. I can recall a brief moment where nothing happened. I thought they had come to their senses.

I was dazed and in pain. I hoped that was the end of the torture.

Seconds later I felt a metal prod around my groin. Then, they started electrocuting me with what must have been a cattle prod.

The pain caused by the electrocution varied in severity.

It actually depended on how long the police held the prod against my body and the strength of the current, which they were turning up and down.

I screamed out in pain. I hoped that someone would hear me, but no one came.

When you are being tortured, you are overcome by a surreal sense of disbelief. You keep hoping that it will stop but when you realize you are trapped, you begin to cope with the pain. This means that to get the desired effect, your torturer has to administer more and more pain.

None of them had spoken during the torture session. Now, their silence was broken by the Captain who asked me if the prod had hurt.

'What do you think? Of course it fucking hurt!' I roared.

They all laughed.

'No, no, my friend,' said the voice. 'That didn't hurt. But this will.'

They gave me a few more jolts with the cattle prod, only this time they increased the voltage. The pain was unbearable.

A few hours ago I had been sitting in the Captain's office drinking beer with the officers and being congratulated for catching O'Connor. Now they were torturing me and laughing about it.

They zapped me a couple of times more, then they started to ask me again, 'Why did you kill your friend? Where did you hide the body? We know you are a killer! Now tell us why!'

I screamed for help. I tried to explain that I hadn't killed anybody. I'd been fighting with O'Connor's bodyguard, but he wasn't dead. He'd run off.

Every time I gave an answer they didn't like, they electrocuted me with the cattle prod again.

After a while they began targeting the more sensitive parts of my body.

They pulled up my t-shirt and zapped me in the stomach, around the nipples and around the side of my chest. When this didn't work, they began electrocuting my groin and my testicles.

The electric shock went right through me. Even my teeth hurt. It was unbelievable and unbearable. My muscles contracted every time I was zapped. I could feel the current in every part of my body.

All the time they kept firing questions at me. It went on and on. When they finally stopped, the officer behind me started to massage my shoulders. He told me that I was very strong, but it would be better for me if I confessed.

I wouldn't confess to anything, especially not to murder!

Everybody has heard stories about police brutality and the third degree treatment, but this was torture – pure and simple.

They then left me alone for a short while. I remember that somebody came in and out of the room at this point. I was still blindfolded but I could hear the door and I could hear them whispering.

Suddenly, without a word, they grabbed hold of me and held me tightly down in the chair. The next thing I knew, they put a plastic bag over my head and pulled it tight at the back of my neck.

I began to struggle. I couldn't breathe! I kept on struggling but it was no use.

The grip on the plastic bag was released a little, which allowed me to breathe again.

They asked the same questions.

'Why did you kill your friend? We know you killed him!'

Again I answered that I didn't know what they were talking about. I said I hadn't killed anyone.

The grip on the plastic bag was pulled tight again, and I struggled to breathe. They knew I was holding my breath as much as I could, so they punched me a couple of times on the side of the face to make sure it was difficult for me.

I was sure my lungs were going to burst any second.

Then I blacked out. I don't know how long I was unconscious for, but they brought me round with a bucket of cold water.

One of the police team slapped me a couple of times across the face to make sure I was fully conscious again. Then they said, 'Now we kill you. You make too many problems for us.'

One of them produced a gun and put it to my head, and slowly began to pull the trigger. I could hear it.

'Say you killed or we kill you! Confess, say you killed!' came the voice in my ear.

Struggling was useless now. They had a strong grip on me and I didn't have enough energy left to fight them.

'Say you killed or we kill you! If you don't confess you die like your friend!'

'It's very easy,' said the Captain. 'We say you tried to escape, so we shot you. No problem.'

The gun was shoved into my temple.

'Now we kill you for sure!'

'Say you killed!'

Again and again I tried to tell them that I hadn't killed anyone, but they just ignored me.

If they wanted to kill me there was nothing that I could do to stop them. I didn't want to die, but I accepted that it was about to happen.

But I was not going to confess.

When they realised that I had accepted that I was going to die and I no longer cared what they did, they began to beat me once again.

One of them grabbed me in a headlock. They placed a plastic bag over my head again, only this time the air was forced out completely, leaving the plastic clinging to my face.

This time, they'd grabbed me so fast that I had no time to prepare myself or catch my breath. In only seconds I was struggling once more for air. I could feel myself slipping. This time I was going to die.

* * *

I had held out, but at that moment in time, if they had promised to free me, I would have admitted to killing John F. Kennedy. Nobody wants to die; the human mind will do anything to keep itself alive. They had tortured me for about five hours, but I felt as if I'd been tortured for days.

Every man has a breaking point, and I had reached mine. I couldn't take it any more; I would have done anything for this nightmare to stop.

They had broken me.

'Okay, okay!' I screamed. 'Whatever you want!'

They never said a word. They just removed the plastic bag and the blindfold.

I felt an enormous sense of relief, but also dread. I wasn't sure if they were going to attack me again.

I was temporarily blinded by the sudden rush of light, but I was soon able to make out what was around me. I couldn't believe what I saw.

O'Connor was in the room. He had watched the police torturing me. He was sitting there, smiling at me.

At that point I wanted to die. I had always believed that I was right to have pursued O'Connor. Now I questioned myself and every decision I had made in the past few years. What had I done?

This feeling of utter desolation got even worse when I noticed a video camera mounted on a tripod in the corner of the room. The bastards had filmed the whole thing with O'Connor.

'What the fuck are you doing?' I asked the guy behind the camera.

He smiled and said, 'Training. We use this film for training.'

They planned to use the footage of me being tortured to teach other cops how to inflict similar pain.

As I said, everyone has their breaking point and this was mine. At that point, I gave up hope.

The police eyed me cautiously. One of them told me they would give me a statement and I must sign it. I said I would do whatever they said. They looked at each other in surprise.

I was next taken over to sit at a table. The cop who'd been behind me during the torture session was now behind me again.

He started massaging my shoulders. I'd still know his touch even to this day.

I was very strong, he told me. Normally 20 minutes is enough. Five hours was the new record.

I felt sick. It was all a game to them. This man was a sadistic bastard.

Next, the confession was brought in. It consisted of a few pages, and was written out entirely in Thai.

I was told where to sign and I signed. Once I had scribbled down my name, my world totally collapsed.

I knew that I had just signed my life away but I didn't care. I was a broken man.

As soon as I signed, I was taken out of the room into a large open area. I was put behind a table with O'Connor and several police officers. We all stood there for only a moment. Then TV crews rushed in with reporters, who screamed questions at me.

I didn't know what was happening. I was in a daze, not having got over the trauma of being tortured. I was confused.

I don't remember what questions they asked or who answered. I only remember one reporter asking, 'Did you kill him?'

I didn't answer. I pointed at O'Connor and said, 'He stole my money. That's all I can remember.'

The press conference only lasted a few minutes but had the desired effect. They allowed photographers to take some shots before whisking me away.

I noticed that my wrists were cut where the handcuffs had bit into the flesh. It had probably happened during the electric shock torture, but I hadn't felt it before.

Now my whole body was in agony. My hands were shaking and every muscle and nerve in my body was on fire.

I couldn't feel anything in my right hand; it was completely numb. I guessed that where the handcuffs pierced my flesh, they must have damaged a nerve. It was three weeks before the feeling came back.

Next, I was put into a room by myself.

A few hours later, at about 11 p.m., the police from Chonburi came to see me. They said they were going to take me to Chonburi, and that tomorrow they'd take me to where the fight with Holdsworth had taken place.

I was manhandled into the front seat of their car and driven to Chonburi town that same night.

It was some time after midnight when we arrived and I was taken to the police suprintendent's office.

The superintendent ordered some sandwiches, and gave me a tin of beer. He apologised that it was only a local beer, and asked if the police in Bangkok had tortured me. I didn't trust him, but I was desperate.

I showed him my wrists and my chest, and explained what they'd done to me for five hours.

'Yes,' he said. 'The tourist police in Bangkok are very, very bad. But don't worry. I do not use those methods.'

Then he smiled.

He introduced himself as Aneke. He spoke good English. He then brought me to a holding cell which housed about 60 Thai and Burmese prisoners. I was the only European among them.

In pain and exhausted, I found a place on the floor and tried to get some sleep. It wasn't easy, but I was exhausted, and I finally fell into a deep sleep. I prayed silently to myself as I lay on the floor. I would have done anything to be at home with my wife and child but it was too late for that now. My life was to change forever.

In the morning I was taken back to Aneke's office. I was given coffee and some biscuits. About half an hour later two men arrived.

Aneke said that these men had something to discuss with me. Holdsworth, he told me, was dead.

7

I was taken to a room to meet the two men. I thought they had come from the Irish embassy but I was wrong. They were dressed formally and introduced themselves as officials from the New Zealand embassy.

I wouldn't have believed anything the police said, but these officials confirmed that they'd just finished identifying the body. Holdsworth really was dead – and I was accused of his murder.

I was astounded. I had signed a confession admitting the murder. Now they had the body. I went into shock.

The officials asked me if I was all right and whether they could do anything to help. The only thing I could think of was to ask them to call my embassy. The situation was now spiralling out of control. I knew I needed help.

I asked the two officials how Holdsworth had died. They looked at me for a moment, then said, 'We'll have to wait for the doctor's report before we'll know the cause of death, but it's clear that Mr Holdsworth had been in a fight.'

'You really didn't know he was dead?' asked Superintendent Aneke.

'How *would* I know?' I answered. 'I've told you I had a fight with him, but I certainly didn't kill him!'

'Maybe you hit him too hard,' said Aneke.

He could see that I was stunned. I had really thought it was only a game O'Connor was playing to put me in prison with him. Now I had to believe that Holdsworth really had been killed. But still, I couldn't believe that I'd been responsible for his death.

Nothing made sense. After the fight, O'Connor had used the spotlight in his car to try and find Holdsworth, but we couldn't find him.

I thought that he'd run away.

I went through the entire thing in my head over and over again.

Could someone else have killed him? Could he have been dazed or disorientated and run out in front of a car?

Could he have died later from concussion or something? Could I have hit him too hard, like Aneke said?

It didn't help that nobody could tell me how or where he'd died. But if the police didn't know how he'd died, how could they accuse me of his murder?

But I was trapped in Bangkok, where anything was possible.

Strangely, all I could think of was O'Connor and how our situations had changed. He had been the one under arrest; I hadn't. I hadn't even been handcuffed. I'd just had him arrested for fraud and theft. He was supposed to be the one facing 15 to 20 years.

I went through every possible scenario.

I thought that someone must have told him that Holdsworth was dead after he had been arrested. Either that or O'Connor lied about not being able to see the bodyguard with the spotlight, and for some bizarre reason kept it to himself.

The truth was that nothing made sense.

I was confused and frightened for the first time in my adult life. I knew I was in serious trouble.

The police chief Aneke sensed this. When the embassy officials left, he took me into his office, sat me down and told me to relax.

He said he had also interviewed O'Connor but thought he was a real criminal and lying through his teeth. He then made me an offer.

He said that if I had 300,000 baht, he would give me bail. In reality, he was saying that he wanted me to pay him in return for letting me go. If I skipped bail, he'd be able to keep the cash.

He was speaking with a forked tongue.

I told him I didn't have that much money. He said I should try to find it. I still to this day don't know whether he was taking advantage of the situation or actually trying to help me.

But as he showed me the door, he told me to get the money from somewhere. He said that most probably, my life depended on it.

I was taken to the cells, where I was held for the next two days with the 60 other prisoners. There were only two cells – one male, one female – and both were packed full.

I was allowed to receive a phonecall from my sister in Ireland.

She noticed almost straight away that I wasn't able to talk properly; I'd had my lip split during the fight with Holdsworth and bitten the inside of my own mouth during the five hours of torture.

She was very distraught and kept asking me if I was really okay. It was obvious that I'd been beaten.

My younger brother also called me. He couldn't believe that I'd been accused of murder.

The Irish embassy came on the scene at this point. They rang to say they had called a lawyer in Bangkok on my behalf. I was told to hang on until the lawyer could meet me.

That afternoon the tourist police from Bangkok arrived once more. I was now terrified of them.

'We go to make a movie,' one of them said. They all seemed to find this very funny, but I knew they weren't joking. They actually wanted to take me to the scene of the fight. They said they wanted me to show them what had happened.

* * *

I had started to cling to the hope that a lawyer would completely destroy any case levied against me, but I quickly began to realise that Thai law is unlike any other. There are plenty of rules and legal safeguards, but nobody follows them. In effect, it's the law of the jungle.

I called the lawyer appointed by the Irish embassy and he said I should do what the police said as it might help prove my innocence. I had never heard of anything like this but I reluctantly agreed. I continually expected the police to free me at any moment. I suppose I convinced myself that everything would be okay, because I couldn't cope if I started to think about what might happen.

Some hours later, I was driven to where they said the fight had taken place. O'Connor was already there waiting with the tourist police when I arrived. He looked fine and unperturbed.

Among the police and detectives gathered at the scene were several camera crews and photographers. This was all bizarre.

O'Connor had taken them precisely to the location where the fight had taken place.

When I looked closely, I could see where Holdsworth and I had slid down the embankment from the road while fighting.

The embankment itself was higher than I'd remembered it, about two or three metres deep. At the bottom of the bank, I saw a six-metre area of grass that was flattened where we'd fought and rolled around.

The signs of a struggle were all there, and a few blades of grass had spots of blood on them, but no more than you'd get if you cut yourself shaving. There was certainly nothing that might indicate someone had been killed.

The police captain from Bangkok who'd supervised my torture session was in charge.

He told me where and how to stand. Then he shouted, 'Action!' and they all started taking photographs and filming.

Mentally broken, I decided to comply with their instructions. I was still afraid. More than anything, I feared that I could be tortured again, or even murdered. The threat was very real.

Standing at the scene of the fight, I watched the police put the finishing touches to their conspiracy.

I knew from the way they conducted themselves that they had told the local press that I had already confessed and was voluntarily showing them how I'd actually murdered Brett Holdsworth.

When I didn't move or do as I was told, the chief would say, 'You remember the plastic bag? Do everything just as you're told – or I'll take you back to Bangkok!'

I could remember bits and pieces of the fight – a punch here, a headbutt there, but there was a lot that I just couldn't recall. I suppose I had blanked it out.

Because of this, I did as I was told and posed here and there as instructed. I did not want to be subjected to more torture.

At one point, I did ask where the bodyguard was supposed to have been killed. There was no cordoned-off area or police tape anywhere. I was told to shut up.

Once the police had taken their photographs and finished filming the scene, I was returned to the holding cells in Chonburi police station.

But just when I thought that my situation couldn't get any worse, I was taken from the cell and directed to an empty meeting room.

I was left sitting there alone and handcuffed for a few minutes when I was joined by the police chief Aneke, and another man and a woman. They were Westerners.

The woman looked at me and started screaming.

'Is that him?'

'Yes,' said Aneke.

At that, the woman physically attacked me.

'You bastard! You killed my brother! I hope you rot in hell, you piece of shit!'

She was hysterical. I thought she was going to try and rip my face apart. Her husband tried to calm her down to no avail.

The man was clearly upset and didn't look like he was in control of his emotions either. He didn't say a word, but glared at me.

I remember thinking that he was built like a rugby player – and I was handcuffed and sitting right beside a second-floor window. I realised I could be thrown through the window to my death at any minute. I didn't need anyone to tell me that the police wouldn't try to stop him. If I was lucky and the glass didn't kill me, the fall would.

Eventually the woman calmed down, and said, 'I want to know why!'

She was now weeping uncontrollably.

I knew there was no point in trying to explain everything from the beginning, so I just told her the truth.

First, I hadn't killed her brother or anyone else. Second, her brother had tried to kill me. I told her that I did have a fight with her brother, but I hadn't seen him since.

I told her that I'd been tortured and I'd now been told he was dead.

Finally I told her that I was deeply sorry for her loss – but I hadn't killed Holdsworth.

The woman looked at Superintendent Aneke and asked, 'I thought you said that he'd confessed?'

Superintendent Aneke just smiled.

'Yes,' he said. 'That's what the tourist police tell me.'

I found the entire situation very uncomfortable. It was also dangerous and humiliating. I asked to be taken back to the cell.

Superintendent Aneke told an officer to take me back to the room where the tourist police were waiting. They gave me some documents to sign – O'Connor's charge sheet etc.

As it happened, O'Connor's passport was sitting on the table, so I reached over and picked it up. This wasn't the passport O'Connor had shown me. And the number was different.

I asked the police if they'd checked to see if it was a fake.

My wife Nanglung came to visit me around this time. She told me she had moved out of the house we'd been renting, and was staying with her mother.

She asked me if I'd told the police about her brothers' involvement. I said that I hadn't and she begged me not to.

She said that if I even mentioned their names to the police, then they'd be arrested too. I promised I wouldn't mention them.

It wasn't as if they'd actually done anything anyway. It wouldn't really serve any purpose to bring them into it.

Looking back now, it was clear that Nanglung wasn't concerned about me. She didn't love me; our marriage was one of convenience for her. I knew this, but she was my only lifeline to the outside world; she was someone who could communicate with the outside world on my behalf.

At that moment in time, this was all that mattered to me.

I stayed at the police station for three more days. There was no more questioning and, thankfully, no more torture.

In fact, Superintendent Aneke treated me very well. He took me into his office every morning for a coffee and most afternoons or evenings he'd give me a beer or two – to help me sleep.

I later concluded that he was really only talking to me to improve his English.

I spent over two weeks in the Siriacha police station in downtown Chonburi. Although the conditions in the holding cells were inhuman by European standards, they were luxurious compared to what was coming next. On 5 August of that same year, I was taken to court on suspicion of murder, where a judge sent me to one of the most squalid and dangerous prisons on earth.

8

The Thai justice system is corrupt to the core. Criminals can buy their way out of any charge if they have the right connections and enough money. There is, to put it simply, no justice.

I had never seen the inside of a Thai courtroom. I knew petty corruption among government officials was rife, but I had no idea that such criminality and corruption was endemic.

The police in Chonburi transported me to court in the back of a pick-up truck. On arrival at the court building I was ushered into a small room, where I was searched.

One of the guards told me to take my shoes and socks off. I looked at the floor. It was soaking wet from where the single toilet had overflowed. There were bits of food, shit and garbage everywhere. And they wanted me to walk barefoot in it.

After a sharp jab in the ribs with a baton, I decided it would be safer to follow orders, and took my shoes and socks off. It was disgusting.

Once I'd entered the cell I noticed that everyone was wearing rusty chains on their legs. I saw three foreigners sitting in the far corner, away from the Thai prisoners. I walked over to them and introduced myself. They might speak English, at least. One of the prisoners introduced himself as Bruno.

'What's the story with the leg irons?' I asked.

'Get used to it. Every time you come to court you have to wear them.'

He said he had been in jail for over two years, so I guessed he must be familiar with the system.

I noticed that a couple of the Thai prisoners had clean, shiny chains, so I asked Bruno why they were not wearing rusty shackles like everyone else.

Bruno laughed and explained that the guys with the clean chains were charged with murder. He said murder suspects had to wear leg irons 24 hours a day until after their trial was over.

He then asked me what I'd been charged with.

'Murder,' I sighed.

'Not to worry,' he said. 'They'll take them off as soon as your trial's over.'

'How long will that take?' I asked.

'About four or five years,' he said matter-of-factly.

I didn't believe a word of it. I thought he was just winding me up. I asked a few more questions about the court and the prison but I didn't believe any of the answers.

Eventually my name was called, and I joined a group of another 20 or so prisoners. I was marched barefoot out of the cell and up to the courtroom on the first floor.

A clerk walked in, called out everyone's name, and then said, 'Remanded for 12 days.'

That was it. There was no judge present, no remand hearing and no defence lawyer.

Shackled, still injured and suffering from shock, I was next told to sign some papers, and then we were all marched back down to the holding cell.

The documents were written in Thai, which I couldn't understand. Although I didn't know what I'd signed, I knew it was a case of either sign or suffer another beating.

Back downstairs in the holding cell, we waited for hours until everything was finished in the court upstairs. The bus came to take us to Chonburi Prison.

This was it: I was actually going to jail.

Looking back, I remember saying to myself that someone would turn up and get me out. The whole thing was a misunderstanding. I was subconsciously trying to convince myself that I would be saved.

After all, I needed something to believe in. I had been tortured, I had signed a murder confession and I was now at the mercy of a justice system run by criminals.

I remember thinking about my family in Ireland and about this nightmare situation as I lined up in the dirt to board the bus. The scene reminded me of documentaries I'd seen about concentration camps in World War II.

As the guy in front stood up, I followed and was counted as I passed out of the cell. The prison bus itself was built to hold a maximum of about 50 men, with a single row of wooden benches running down each side, and standing room in the middle.

On that particular day, the guards beat, pushed and shoved at least 120 prisoners into the vehicle. I had never experienced anything like it.

I was pinned solid between 120 stinking bodies. Someone was standing on my feet, someone else's elbow was digging into my back, while someone's shoulder was lodged in my throat.

I was barely able to move. The bus had no glass in the windows, just bars and a wire mesh. The heat was stifling.

We were treated like animals. The driver was totally unconcerned about his human cargo. He drove at speed and often had to brake hard for a corner. This would result in the passengers surging forward, squashing each other.

You couldn't fall because there just wasn't anywhere to fall. We were jammed together and held each other up.

I vividly remember entering the jail. We were unloaded in an open yard about 20 metres square. It was here that the real brutality began.

Shackled and chained, we were unloaded off the bus. The seasoned prisoners were lined up in rows. There were about 15 new prisoners with me, and we were lined up to the side.

All the prisoners stripped off their shirts and opened the string holding their shorts. I didn't know what to do and just followed the others' lead.

I was trying to stay alive and blend in. I was convinced that I would be killed if a row broke out.

The guards were all ex-army paratroopers. They looked like military men. They wore fatigues, complete with parachute wings, campaign badges and combat boots, and they carried heavy wooden batons – two or three inches think, and three feet long.

Everyone referred to them as the commandos. There were about six of them in charge of us that particular day.

Some of the guards wore what looked like security guards' uniforms, but with shorts instead of long trousers. These also carried batons.

I would learn that these guards were trustees, or blueshirts. They were prisoners who acted as junior guards.

They were all menacing characters and, by the looks of them, they were capable of anything.

One commando walked through the rows of prisoners, stopping at each man, and forcing him to open his mouth and stick out his tongue. This guard peered into each man's mouth to make sure he hadn't concealed anything.

Each prisoner was then forced to let his shorts fall to the ground and expose himself. The commando forced every one of us to lift our penises and testicles, and then pull back our foreskins.

What seemed to be a ritual humiliation didn't end there. He next made each one of us turn around, bend over, and pull our buttocks apart to let another commando search inside our anuses. Each man repeated this as the guard walked along the line.

Anyone slow at performing this task was beaten.

The commandos hated the prisoners. There was something sinister about the way they moved among us. I couldn't make out what it was at first but it was there.

They never made eye contact or spoke to the prisoners; I can only describe them as being inhuman.

In time I would learn that they made a point of ritually degrading a small number of prisoners at every opportunity in order to keep us under control. On that day, they picked two or three out of each line and they were told to stand to one side for no apparent reason.

The new prisoners were the last group subjected to this ordeal that particular day. We were told to strip naked right there, and leave our clothes in a pile in front of us. I did as I was told.

A trustee then came and checked our clothes and any belongings. No long trousers or jeans were allowed, so mine were cut to make shorts. The trustees also removed our jewellery and watches.

I quickly realised that if a commando liked a watch, he simply took it. If the commando liked a ring, he also took it.

As we were standing there, one guy was stupid enough to protest when the commando picked up a particularly expensive-looking gold watch. The guy said it had been a present from his mother; he really couldn't bear to give it away.

The commando looked at him, dropped the watch and crushed it with the heel of his combat boot. If he couldn't have it, nobody else could either.

One by one, we paraded naked in front of a commando who was sitting down. This man was a chief. He asked what we were charged with. We answered individually. He next pointed at our groins with his stick.

We lifted our penises and testicles, pulled back our foreskins, turned, bent over and he checked our rectums. It was humiliating.

The other prisoners stood laughing at our embarrassment and awkwardness. 100-odd people laughing at us compounded the appalling experience.

But it wasn't over. He picked me and two other men out of the 15 new prisoners and told us to go and stand with the others he'd picked out earlier. I was among the chosen few.

As I stood there, still naked, a trustee came over with a bucket of water and a bar of soap. He told us to soap our behinds as he put on a rubber glove.

The first man in line obeyed him without question; he soaped his arse and bent over. The trustee thrust two or three fingers into the prisoner's anus.

He pulled his fingers out after a few seconds, rinsed his hand in the bucket and moved on to the next man, and then the next. I was about fifth in line.

When he came to me, the trustee said, 'Hey you, foreigner. You're next.'

I told him to fuck off.

The commando calmly walked towards me.

'What did you say?'

I told him that I was not going to allow anyone to search me internally. I said I didn't care what they did: nobody was going to put their fingers up my arse. As soon as I opened my mouth I began to panic. I feared I would be raped, or worse.

Trying desperately to think of a legitimate way of backing down, I pointed out that the trustee had used the same glove on the other prisoners but had only rinsed his hands in water. I said the risk of catching AIDS was more than I was willing to accept.

I told the commando that if he wanted to check my rectum I couldn't stop him, but asked if he could get a doctor.

I knew the commando would have to beat me for insubordination, but I made up my mind not to make it easy for him. I have moments of bravery, or stupidity, and at that moment I didn't care if I got beaten or shot dead.

The commando smiled, hit me hard in the stomach, and walked away.

I was surprised and more than a little relieved. The trustee moved on down the line and carried out his revolting instructions. Everyone else obeyed without question, but I managed to escape the internal search.

9

The prisoners were counted and led off to their cells. Of the new prisoners, I was the only one charged with murder, so I was taken to the chain shop.

Two commandos and four trustees escorted me to a small room located in the prison basement. The chain shop was like something out of the middle ages.

They made me sit on a chair in front of an anvil. The 'chain man', a prisoner, carefully selected a set of chains with ankle rings. They weighed about 4 kg and were dirty, rusty old ones.

Two of the trustees held me down while another two lifted my leg and held it on the anvil. The chain man slipped the ankle ring over my feet and hammered it closed. I was manhandled like a wild animal.

Now I was shackled. I think this experience affected me more than any other. I felt like a slave; I was overcome with a sense of utter desolation and despair.

I refused to pick up the chains and walk. On one hand I kept saying to myself that I wasn't a fucking animal and I wasn't going to accept being chained like one.

In reality, the chains represented the end of my life as I knew it. I had not only lost my liberty but also my self belief. You could say the chains represented my innermost horror.

In fact, it was so bad that I couldn't bear to touch them, or even look at my feet. Instead, I shuffled away, dragging the chains along behind me because I refused to accept that I was manacled.

Once chained, I was escorted into a cell used to hold those returning from court.

The cell looked full, but the commando opened the door and shoved me in anyway. I stood there in despair, not knowing what to do until the room leader came over to me.

He spoke very basic English.

'What your name? How old you? You killing case?'

The latter was obvious – I was in chains.

This man showed me some kindness in what I considered to be my darkest hour.

'You sleep here, okay my friend?'

He pointed me towards an empty space on the floor.

There was no bed, mattress, or blanket. There was just a cold and hard concrete floor.

There were over 100 Thai prisoners in the cell, and they all slept shoulder to shoulder. Some were lucky enough to have blankets to lie on, but most didn't.

Even though the cell became a sort of refuge it was still utterly squalid.

There were three open-style toilets which were really just holes in the ground, and a large earthenware jar full of water which was used both for drinking and for flushing the toilet. There was no toilet paper. The prisoners used their hands to clean themselves, then washed themselves in the water jar.

One of my friends had brought me a book when I was in the police station. I remember that it was written by Wilbur Smith and called *A Sparrow Falls*. I used it as my pillow.

I didn't sleep on my first night.

The sensation of wearing chains made it very difficult to relax or find any kind of comfortable position to rest. What I found upsetting was the fact that the chains didn't actually serve a purpose other than to degrade.

They left prisoners with a sense of total imprisonment, and total defeat.

I lay awake all that night thinking about everything that had happened to me. I cried myself to sleep. I dreaded what horrors awaited me in the morning.

But I also promised myself that I would survive no matter what I had to do. I had reached rock-bottom, which presented me with two options. I could either put an end to my life, or I could stay alive and try to secure my freedom.

* * *

In the morning I was taken to see the building chief. He only spoke Thai, so a Pakistani prisoner called Ali was brought along to translate.

The building chief asked me about my case. I explained what had happened as best I could.

The first question my new chief asked was, 'Why didn't you pay?'

In fact, every Thai prisoner, every prison guard and every lawyer would ask this.

'If you'd paid you wouldn't be here. It's the same,' he said. 'The police call it bail but it's the same. It goes straight into their pockets. It's better to pay! Now you will have to pay the prosecutor too, maybe half a million baht. If you don't pay, you will lose.'

In Thailand it's not so much that paying off the police is an option, it's expected.

After my interview with the building chief, Ali showed me around – not that there was much to see.

The ethos of Chonburi was all about degradation and keeping the prisoners contained. The facilities were primitive and dilapidated.

There was a block of ten open toilets that were used by 2,000 prisoners. The shower area was fenced off with barbed wire. The showers, though, were not showers at all. They consisted of large water troughs that you scooped water from with a bowl.

Ali told me that prisoners were only allowed five bowls of water each. The guards would whistle and you'd take one. If you tried to take another or if your timing was out, they'd beat you with a club.

Ali then took me to the prison shop where the commandos sold food, and finally to the canteen itself, where the prisoners were supposed to eat.

He told me that the daily dish was red rice, doled out of large vats with a shovel, and a spicy fish-bone soup; which contained no fish meat.

I got close enough to smell it, and that was all I dared to do.

The Thai prisoners, Ali told me, all worked in the prison factories from eight in the morning until eight at night, with an hour for lunch.

Most of the factories were assembly-type work areas where they made umbrellas, plastic flowers and paper bags. There was also a woodwork shop which produced furniture.

Ali explained that each prisoner was given a quota which he must complete – for example, 20 umbrellas or 50 plastic flowers per hour. If the prisoner failed to reach his quota, he would be beaten by the guards, so most people paid for the more experienced inmates to slip them a few of theirs.

Or, as Ali pointed out, inmates could pay off a guard each month to leave them alone.

Money talked.

The idea and principle of having inmates work, apart from occupying them, was to give the inmates a little income so that they could support themselves.

Some of the factories in Chonburi were government sponsored, mostly producing fancy goods or artwork.

I learned that inmates working in these factories were paid up to 500 baht per month – not a large sum, but enough to buy a few necessities.

The other factories, though, were controlled by the prison. An individual or a company paid the prison for the use of one of the factories and the inmates. This was slave labour, pure and simple.

The guard in charge of that factory charged commission on everything his factory produced. The salary for working in one of these factories was ten to 20 baht a month. That's about 80 cents.

The money for the salaries was paid to the prison, but Ali informed me that the commandos and guards stole most of it and divided it amongst themselves, leaving a pittance for their slave labourers.

I was flabbergasted; I couldn't believe what I was hearing.

But at this point I finally heard some good news.

Foreigners didn't work, Ali told me – not because they're not supposed to, but because they refuse.

Whispering in my ear, he told me not to agree to work under any circumstances. He said there was absolutely no regard for safety. There were no work clothes or overalls, and in most of the factories there weren't even benches or work tables. Everybody sat and worked on the floor.

So all foreigners refused to work and sat in the canteen all day, or simply walked around the prison yard. He said I should do the same. I agreed.

* * *

The prison regime was based on the principle that prisoners should be treated like animals. The prison rules made no sense whatsoever.

As I began to see what life inside was going to be like, Ali told me that sport is only allowed after working hours.

But foreigners weren't even allowed to lift weights. He said the commandos claimed that we were too big already and they didn't want us getting any bigger or stronger.

Thai prisoners, on the other hand, were allowed to pump iron all day if they wanted.

I'd always considered myself to be an open minded and enlightened person. After all, by that time I'd done a lot of travelling, so I thought I'd seen most that human nature had to offer.

But that day I began to realise that in a Thai prison, all standards and normal codes of behaviour go out the window.

When I was locked into my cell at night, I gradually came to conclude that I had been jailed with a group of animals.

After a few days, my fellow prisoners began to disgust me. They picked their noses while talking to others. One man used every finger on his hand to pick his nose until he finally got the piece of snot he wanted, and then ate it, all while talking face to face with his friends.

It was horrific and turned my stomach.

In the cell, prisoners would often sit down beside me and squeeze their spots and pimples. They would also repeat this practice in the canteen where they would wipe the pus on the dinner table, or chair.

It got worse.

During the first week, I saw some of them sit down and, in full view of everyone, take their penises out and compare them, check their pubic hair for lice, then smell their fingers.

I saw one man scratch his armpit with his spoon, next scratch his arse with it before using the spoon to eat his lunch.

I also saw prisoners swapping spit with their boyfriends as if they hadn't a care in the world.

They used to blow their noses out onto the floor. It was like something from hell.

The amount of snot that can come out of one person's nose is unbelievable. The same goes for spitting. You couldn't walk in the cell without stepping in someone's snot or spit. They had no sense of respect for others.

During the first week, I remember standing at the water trough trying to have a shower.

Minutes later, I noticed that the man next to me was pissing on my feet. There was no hygiene, never mind honour among thieves.

I quickly came to realise that it was the law of the jungle that ruled within Chonburi.

For example, fighting was an everyday occurrence at shower time. Men would push and beat each other senseless for a jug of water. The commandos never intervened because fights were considered a form of entertainment.

The atmosphere sent me into a spiral of depression.

I had difficulties with everything. I began to lose weight because I couldn't find any sort of edible food inside the jail.

My other problem involved going to the toilet. There were no toilets that flushed. As I said, the toilets consisted of a hole in the ground, which no one cleaned. It was rancid, and the smell was disgusting.

I put off going to the toilet for as long as I could, but two days after I first arrived I realised I had to bite the bullet.

The first time I tried to relieve myself, I vomited.

Eventually I attempted to go only to have another prisoner come right up to me.

'You got a cigarette, my friend?'

I soon learned that, for some reason, Thai prisoners love to hang around, eat and even play chess directly in front of other prisoners while they're trying to use the toilets.

On that occasion, I had to stop. I tried to relieve myself the next day but I was unable to. Have you ever tried to use a toilet with a room full of people watching you? I certainly couldn't.

I quickly learned that decency and dignity were dirty words in Chonburi. Nobody even pretended, because there was no point.

Nothing I'd ever experienced prepared me for life inside a Thai prison. It was hell on earth.

The frustration and despair I felt was overwhelming. I found depression impossible to avoid, especially because I was kept chained like an animal 24 hours a day.

In those first few days, I became fixated on myself and everything about me. I fixated on the chains.

Dragging them around between my legs was my way of rebelling against the system. It was my way of protesting.

But after a few days, I couldn't even walk. Every time I attempted to move, I kept tripping over, but I still refused to pick them up.

I became more depressed as the days passed. I would secretly cry at night and wallow in my own misery. I could see no way out and contemplated suicide.

The chains became my obsession. They seemed to affect every facet of my life.

I couldn't wash properly with them on. It was impossible to take my shorts off, so I'd shower, still wearing them, and then stumble around, or sit in the sun until they dried.

My chains had been dirty when they were hammered on, but after a few days of showering in them and dragging them around they were putrid. This added to my despair.

Then someone showed me some kindness.

One of the other foreign prisoners, Stefan from Germany, came and talked to me. Stefan had been in chains for nearly three years, and he explained that I'd better get used to it. He encouraged me to pull myself together.

He laid it on the line. He said the chains wouldn't be taken off until after I had been sentenced, whether I liked it or not.

If I fought my case that meant at least five years, he said. And if I was sentenced to 30 years or more, they wouldn't come off at all.

More than 30 years? At the time I couldn't contemplate the idea of spending the rest of my life in Chonburi. It was too much for me.

Stefan showed me how to change my shorts while wearing shackles and how to scrub and clean them to avoid infections from the dirt and rust.

I now dedicated myself to keeping them spotlessly clean. The shackles were made of mild steel, so new rust would form every day. It took about six months, scrubbing every day, to get them really clean. There weren't any Brillo pads or special cleaners, only soap and elbow grease, but I persevered and they became bearable.

Once I realised that no one was going to come and rescue me, I began to deal with my situation.

By this time I had lost all faith. For a variety of reasons, my own family were not in a position to help in any practical way.

My only hope was that justice would prevail in the courtroom. In this regard, I decided to focus on preparing a solid defence for my trial.

* * *

I was brought to court 12 days later. In the first few days inside that squalid jail, I had hoped and prayed that the Thai courts would somehow become my salvation. But even the experience of going to court was shrouded in brutality and indignity.

When the day came, I was forced to wear the prison-issue brown clothes – brown shirt and brown shorts, no underwear and, of course, no socks or shoes.

I was loaded onto a bus with dozens of men and driven to a courthouse. I half expected them to remove the chains before we entered the court; I thought they would prejudice my trial. But I was wrong.

We were marched into the court only to find that once again there was no judge, no prosecutor and no lawyer. There was only a court clerk and the police. There was no hearing.

The clerk called out all 20 names, and said, '12 days.'

And that was it. The whole process didn't take more than five minutes.

Once again, we were squeezed like sardines onto the bus; we were strip-searched by the sadistic guards; we watched the new prisoners get humiliated; we rushed through into the sleeping section for a very quick shower; and we hurried up to the room to be counted and locked up for the night.

I would go through exactly the same procedure seven times before I was even formally charged.

The police had 84 days to complete their investigations. After that they had to charge you or let you go. I eventually found out that no judge or prosecutor bothered to go to the court before the 84 days had expired.

I convinced myself that I would be released after I had spent 84 days in jail because I had not received any legal papers or been served with any charge sheets.

I talked to my new friends about what I was going to do when I was released. No one contradicted me because I seemed to be in better spirits. The notion of freedom lifted me out of my despair.

I had been taken to court every 12 days and nothing had happened. I interpreted this as a good sign.

When the 84-day period had expired, I was taken to court as usual with everyone else. I was sure this was the day they were going to release me. My mental health had improved noticeably. I was in good form.

After I complied with the various security procedures at the court, I was brought before another court clerk.

He told me to sign for another 12 days. I couldn't believe it; I felt like a fool. I fought back the tears and promised myself I would never be so self-deluding again.

There was nothing I could do. I kept asking myself what was happening. Just as I was being put onto the bus to go back to the prison, a court police guard came up to me.

'You Colin Martin?' he asked.

'Yes. I'm Colin Martin.'

'This is for you,' he said.

He handed me three pages of paper, and simply walked away. At first I thought he had given me release papers or some court order. But the commandos insisted that I step on the bus and return to the prison. I held on to the papers for my dear life.

During the strip-search at the prison gate, one commando saw the papers lying on the ground at my feet while I stood naked.

He asked me what they were.

'I don't know,' I said. 'They're in Thai.'

He held out his hand, so I picked them up and gave the papers to him. He told me that they were my charge papers. I'd just been charged with first degree murder.

10

By the time I was charged with murder, I'd come to terms with the situation that I found myself in. I had pulled myself together as best I could. I suppose I knew all along in my heart that I was trapped and wouldn't be freed any time soon. In this regard, the most important lesson that I learned was that I couldn't survive without money.

Nothing was provided in prison, and nothing was free. The food they gave the prisoners was inedible. To stay alive, I had to buy my own food from the guards along with everything else. So I never knew whether I'd eat tomorrow if I bought food today.

The prison authorities didn't even give me a blanket, razors, soap, a toothbrush, toothpaste, or any of the other necessities I needed to stay clean and healthy. Everything came down to money. I realised that fighting my way through the legal system, too, would take cash.

At that time my older brother and sister sent money when they could afford it, but it wasn't a weekly or monthly amount. If they didn't have money to spare, I didn't eat. I continued to lose weight.

I didn't really worry about my health in the beginning because I didn't think that I'd be in jail very long. When I say long, I mean years. I lived in the hope that I would be freed in the coming months.

Whatever money I had of my own when I was arrested, I'd left with my wife Nanglung. I'd given everything to her and told her to take care of herself and our 18-month-old son Brendan. My older brother Tommy also sent her some money when he could.

Nanglung used to visit me regularly, but I wouldn't let her buy me anything because she had no income. This left me in a horrific position.

But there was worse to come.

Some months after my arrest, my brother Tommy arrived in Thailand with money and medicines. His visit was a relief. He was a lifeline. When he arrived, he immediately began to look for ways to secure my release.

Legally, I was entitled to bail for the duration of my trial. I discussed it with Tommy and he offered to put up the money.

We decided that it would be best to rent the land papers or deeds of a Thai person willing to help. One of the lawyers I had hired had told me that I would be required to pay 20 per cent of the bail bond.

I was told that bail isn't set in Thailand; instead, defendants and their lawyer simply take a guess at what the court will accept. In my case, we thought that one million baht (about $40,000) would be enough, which required a payment of 200,000 baht to rent the land papers.

My lawyer agreed to arrange everything and Tommy offered to pay the money. When Tommy arrived in Thailand, he naturally spent some time with my wife Nanglung. He discussed the bail application with her.

When Tommy said the lawyer would make the bail application, she told me and Tommy not to trust him – she said he'd probably steal the money.

I was paranoid and took her word. She was Thai, and probably more familiar with the system than I was. She said that if I gave her the money she would make the necessary arrangements with her family to rent suitable land papers. Her family were farmers and owned their own land.

I had no reason not to trust her. She was my wife and the mother of my child.

So Tommy arranged to raise the money for bail on his return to Ireland, and promptly sent it. I know that Nanglung went and collected it from the embassy.

That was the last I heard of her. She stole the money and vanished.

I have to admit that I blamed myself as much as anyone else. Our marriage was one of convenience. She was a young and attractive woman who married me simply to provide for her. I always knew this. Young Thai women don't fall in love with older foreigners. They fall in love with the lifestyle we can give them.

She'd never had so much money in her hands in her life, and temptation – or greed – took over.

As a prisoner in Thailand you don't have the right to file charges against anybody unless it's related to your case.

Stealing is stealing, but since my wife wasn't directly involved in my dealings with O'Connor and Holdsworth, there was nothing I could do about it.

At the time, I couldn't comprehend what had happened. I asked myself again and again how on earth I had ended up in this situation. When I wrote to Tommy and told him what had happened, he simply couldn't believe it either.

My family refused to send any more money for bail, and I couldn't really blame them. But I was now completely stuck.

You have no idea how I felt. The anger nearly drove me crazy. I should have stayed in prison for only about five months, then made bail and fought my case from the outside, or better still, returned home.

As I soon found out, what made my situation even more serious was that I would have had a much better chance to beat the murder charge if I'd been out on bail. If a defendant is free it makes a big difference in the eyes of the court.

In practical terms, if a defendant arrives in court dressed smartly in a shirt and tie, the judge gets an opportunity to see him in a positive light. When defendants arrive in shackles and filthy prison uniforms, they are usually convicted. I didn't know until two years later that I was entitled to wear a suit, because nobody told me.

Now I was forced to accept that I would have to stay in that stinking hell hole until my trial ended.

* * *

Looking back on that time, I find it hard to explain how complicated my predicament was. I might as well have had no legal representation.

My lawyer had only been to see me once during the 84 days I'd been in prison. And when we spoke, he expressed no interest in my case. The only thing he seemed interested in was his fee.

I remember him sitting with me and saying that he would charge $20,000, but his fee could double if my case turned out to be complicated. At the time, I didn't have $20,000 or anywhere near it, but I said nothing. I knew he would abandon me if he knew the truth.

The legal consultation was farcical. The only truthful thing he said was that it would take months for my trial to start. And that he would, of course, need a down payment.

For the first time, I decided to start playing them all at their own game. I assured him there would be no trouble in paying his required fees, and promised him I'd try to work something out.

I was sent to court 12 days later.

I assumed that my ploy would work, but when I arrived in court, the lawyer was nowhere to be seen.

I waited and waited in the court holding cell. Eventually my name was called and I was taken upstairs to a courtroom, without a defending lawyer. Evidently, he had no interest in the case until he was paid.

I remember that day for all the wrong reasons. It should have been the beginning of the end of my troubles, but it was actually the day my life took another horrible turn for the worse.

A judge walked in and asked me in Thai how I pleaded. I said that I didn't understand Thai, so the judge sent for a translator. I was taken back downstairs to wait.

The translator arrived two hours later. I still had no lawyer, but there was no prosecutor either. Through the translator, the judge explained that I had been charged with the first degree murder of Mr Brett Holdsworth. He asked me if I had a lawyer. I said I did, so he asked where my lawyer was.

I said I didn't know.

The judge told me that murder was a very serious charge, and that I'd have to have a reliable lawyer. He decided that he would appoint one to defend me, and he set the next court appearance for a date six weeks away. That was it.

* * *

I kept myself together in anticipation of the trial date. I'd been disappointed so much at this stage that I never really allowed my hopes to build up, but I was quietly confident that the new court-appointed lawyer assigned to my case might be more effective than his predecessor.

Six weeks later I was transferred to court, where I met my new lawyer. He introduced himself, was accompanied by a translator, and seemed quite professional. Perhaps that was mainly because he had actually turned up. We had a brief discussion in court while I waited for the judge to arrive. At that point he explained that there would be no hearing.

'You've only been brought to court to meet me,' he said.

'Why couldn't you have come to the prison?' I asked.

He looked at me blankly.

'That's not the way we do things in Thailand.'

My illusions were shattered instantly. He snapped his briefcase shut and bid me a brief farewell before I was returned to jail.

The weeks and months passed without any news from the prosecution. I let matters run their course. I had no other option.

I was transported to court every 12 weeks or so, where I would meet my lawyer. He was no better than the others. After the second hearing, he started to ask for money, and he got very angry when I asked him how I was supposed to raise any cash from behind bars.

I now saw him for what he was. He had only turned up at the court in the hope of receiving an advance payment.

The judge never showed for the remand hearings either. It was all very coincidental. I suspected that since the judge had assigned the lawyer to my case, the two were in it together.

* * *

Later that same year, my wife Nanglung reappeared at one of my court appearances with news. She turned up unexpectedly at the court. To be honest, I didn't know what to say to her when I saw her. I was stunned.

She eventually walked over to me. I engaged in some small talk. I asked about Brendan and how he was coping. She told me he was doing well and missed me very much.

Then she eventually told me the reason why she'd come.

She said she had heard that O'Connor had died three weeks previously in Lard Yao prison in Bangkok. I was doubly shocked.

I thought about this for a moment. I wasn't sure if it was true. I wasn't sure if I trusted Nanglung.

Even if she was telling the truth, I wouldn't necessarily believe that O'Connor really was dead. Maybe he'd paid to fake his own death and disappeared. With enough money, anything is possible in Thailand, especially inside a prison. And O'Connor had plenty of money.

But if it was true, it was good news. Death inside a Thai prison was something I wouldn't wish upon anybody, even O'Connor—but, on the other hand, O'Connor was the one man who had accused me of Holdsworth's murder. If he really was dead, I figured the prosecution would have no case. With no witness, they would have to release me.

Minutes after Nanglung gave me the news, the prosecutor dealing with my case just happened to enter the court. I told my lawyer about O'Connor and asked him to ask his opposite if O'Connor was indeed dead.

He did as he was told, then came back and said the prosecutor didn't know anything about it.

For some reason, my lawyer took it upon himself to find out exactly what had happened. In the space of a few hours, he managed to obtain copies of O'Connor's death certificate. As it turned out, there were two certificates—one for Gerald Cathar O'Connor, an Irish national, and one for a Mitchel Joseph Laddie Heath, a New Zealand national. The dates of birth on each certificate were also different.

In fairness to him, by that afternoon my lawyer had confirmed that O'Connor's true name was Mitchel Heath, and that he was dead.

I guessed that O'Connor had got sick and been unable to recover in the prison.

I thought that I would be free within weeks. My trial would almost certainly collapse.

But I was wrong.

Shortly after the prosecutor left the court, my lawyer went over to an official and collected some papers. I distinctly remember allowing myself to believe for a second that the documents were my release papers. But again, any illusion I had that I would soon be free was soon completely shattered. My lawyer returned to say that O'Connor was due to be the first witness at the next court date.

When I asked the obvious question, he told me the hearing was due to be held in Bangkok in two weeks time because that's where O'Connor was. He then explained, in logic that made sense only to himself, that it would be too much trouble to transport me there and back for just one day, so I wouldn't be allowed to go.

However, he said he would attend the hearing and secure my release. If O'Connor was really dead, he told me, then he would demand that my trial be stopped and the case closed.

'Don't worry,' he said. 'I'll take care of everything!'

Needless to say, when he said, 'Don't worry,' I began to panic.

Six months passed before I was called to court again. Nobody told me what had happened at the hearing in Bangkok and I hadn't heard anything from my own lawyer. The court process was a joke.

When I arrived in the courtroom, the judge sat down and read out what had happened in Bangkok.

My lawyer was present that day but made no eye contact with me. When I was brought into the court-room he had made a point of not looking at me. In fact, he ignored me completely.

The judge proclaimed that Mr O'Connor had failed to turn up to give evidence, before stating that the case would not proceed without this vital witness.

I listened to the speech in utter disbelief.

Next, the judge announced that he was adjourning the trial until 26 June 1998 to another court, where O'Connor would present himself.

My lawyer just sat there and said nothing.

As the hearing seemed to be over, and my lawyer hadn't said anything about O'Connor's death, I stuck my hand up and managed to get the judge's attention. The lawyer looked at me in horror, as did the judge.

I ignored them both and started to explain to the judge that O'Connor was in fact dead.

The judge was astonished that I had spoken. Everybody in the court seemed to be too. The judge did his best to look solemn and asked my lawyer if this was indeed the case.

'Is Mr O'Connor really dead?'

'Yes, it's true, Your Honour,' he said, bowing at the judge. 'Mr O'Connor is dead.'

The judge said nothing, then turned and left the courtroom without saying a word.

'What the hell are you playing at?' I said. 'My case should have been closed if there were no witnesses! Why did you just sit there?'

He didn't say anything. He just looked at me, but his translator was far from silent.

'Rude, ungrateful bastard!' he said. 'He has done everything to help you. He went to Bangkok for the hearing and he's here to help you today, and you insult him by talking directly to the judge!'

I lost my temper and I sacked him right there and then. His translator called me a few names but I didn't care. That was the end of him.

I found a new lawyer, my third since this ordeal began. I hoped he would move to conclude the case as quickly as possible – if only so that he'd get paid quickly.

But my decision to appoint him only delayed my final trial date. It was back to the same old routine. I would be taken from prison to court every 12 weeks just to hang around and wait.

My Thai was still pretty basic at this stage. I was learning but I still had trouble. I only found out what was going on in court through the Thai boys who were on trial during the same sessions. They listened to all the other cases, and reported in detail what had been said. Without them, I wouldn't have known how I was being screwed.

My trial finally came to court after three years. It was a very informal hearing, to say the least.

This time, the prosecution called witnesses.

The first was one of my colleagues, who'd come with me to help at the meeting at the construction yard. He testified that I had explained to him how this Mr O'Connor had stolen $460,000 from me using one of his con tricks. He told the court that he had agreed to help me catch O'Connor and arranged for two Thai policemen to be present at the meeting.

He agreed with my statement that O'Connor had attacked me the moment he realised he'd been caught. He said that O'Connor seemed to be too strong for me and the two police officers had to pull him off me. There had been no further trouble and towards the end of the meeting he'd left, so didn't know what happened after that.

He also testified that he had known me for a couple of years, and described me as a nice guy who was liked by everybody at the office. He and everyone else were surprised to hear that I'd been arrested for murder.

My lawyer didn't bother cross-examining him, because he'd said nothing damaging. In fact, I thought he'd helped the case for the defence more than the prosecution.

The second witness was one of the police officers present at the meeting where I'd caught O'Connor. He testified that he'd been asked to attend and arrest O'Connor when he appeared. This officer said he had seen O'Connor attack me and had dragged him off me.

He said that O'Connor had agreed to return the money he had stolen and he and the other police officer had left.

He said he could shed no light on what might have occurred after that, and he knew nothing about any murder. Again, this prosecutor's witness could tell the court nothing and said nothing that could be or was damaging to me.

The third witness was supposed to be the doctor who'd examined Holdsworth's body. However, he decided not to attend court, but a written report he supplied was entered as evidence by the prosecutor.

The document simply said that it was clear from the marks and bruises on Holdsworth's body that he had been involved in a fight. The report stated that Holdsworth had been stabbed a number of times, and had a gash on his neck and his ear, possibly after having been bitten by a rat or a dog.

The report didn't specifically state the cause of death; it just confirmed that Holdsworth was dead. The case was farcical in almost every way. The prosecution presented no forensic evidence linking me to the crime.

But they saved the best till last.

Towards the end, the prosecutor held up a piece of paper – which he claimed was the murder weapon.

It wasn't a knife; it wasn't even a photograph of a knife. It was a black-and-white photocopy of part of a knife, twisted and bent with no handle.

I thought I was seeing things. I looked around the court to see if the real knife was being examined by anyone or put on display, but I could see nothing.

The prosecutor continued to speak. He said the knife had been found by police, not in, on or near the body, but somewhere in the vicinity of the supposed murder scene.

There were no fingerprints.

I'd been shown this half-a-knife at the police station. It was twisted and bent and rusty, but the police had tried to hammer some of the dents out of it. I remember thinking that they hadn't done a very good job, because the dents were still clear even in the photocopy.

The prosecutor told the judge that traces of blood had been found on the knife. Unfortunately, there wasn't enough to identify the blood group, but he said he was sure it was the victim's blood.

I objected to my lawyer about this piece of paper being accepted as material evidence. I always believed that material evidence means exactly that – the genuine article, not a photograph, and certainly not a photocopy, must be presented in court.

I looked on, wondering when this charade would come to an end. I actually felt confident that the judge would just order a retrial.

I tapped my lawyer on the shoulder and asked him to do something. He turned around and told me it wasn't necessary for him to object. He said the judge would know himself that this wasn't acceptable. If we objected, he said, it would look like we were trying to teach the judge points of law.

He was very anxious that I should keep calm and remain silent.

'Calm down!' he told me. 'If you're angry in front of the judge, he might think you're aggressive. In a murder trial that's not a good idea. If you're not careful it might get you convicted!'

Against my better judgement, I promised to say nothing. I sincerely believed that I was finally about to be freed. I didn't want to do anything to jeopardise that.

The final pieces of evidence the prosecutor placed before the judges were the photographs taken at the police reconstruction, which he claimed showed me re-enacting the murder and also showed my blood-stained clothing.

This was too much. I objected to this without waiting for my lawyer to intervene.

I stood up and proclaimed that the police had taken me to the scene and told me where to stand and what to do, under threat of torture. I wanted the judge to know what happened.

My lawyer looked shocked.

The judge turned in my direction and said, 'But that is you in the photographs, isn't it?'

I confirmed that it was, but before I could object further, the judge got up and left the courtroom. My lawyer sat there with an expressionless face.

When I asked him why he hadn't objected, he said, 'I told you not to make the judge angry!'

I didn't get the opportunity to say anything else. The trial was adjourned yet again and I was returned to prison. As soon as the judge walked out the door, I knew I was fucked.

11

Chonburi Prison was designed to hold 3,500 but it actually held over 5,000, with new arrivals every day.

I often asked myself when they would stop sending men to the already cramped facility. Out of fear, the Thai prisoners never complained, because commandos regularly murdered inmates and raped them. This ensured compliance.

Foreigners were treated slightly better. When I was in Chonburi there were only around 50 foreign inmates, so they considered themselves to have 4,950 submissive inmates, and about 50 problem-causing foreigners.

The commandos never trusted us and were always on their guard when they were around us. They knew that we knew they engaged in all types of crime.

I knew that the prison's director and the guards stole whatever they could. They stole much of what was intended for our basic provisions and divided it among themselves according to ranking. The prisoners were left to fend for themselves.

The place was a cesspit. We were locked up between 3.30 p.m. and 4 p.m. every day. There was no food allowed in the rooms, and no smoking. The only drink allowed was water. There were water bottles in the rooms, but they were filled from the toilet system. Foreigners wouldn't go near this water, so we were forced us to buy fresh drinking water from the guards.

They co-operated with us in supplying water because it earned them money, but that was where the relationship ended. We were granted no extra privileges. We were all thoroughly searched before being allowed into the cell block.

We were permitted to keep no personal belongings in the rooms. If they caught you smuggling cigarettes, you were given a choice. You could either eat them or be taken out and given a vicious beating.

This was usually one punch or kick per cigarette but, depending on the guard on duty, they might also strip you and make you stand spread-eagled for everybody to have a good laugh at. If you were lucky, they'd give you your clothes back that night.

If not, you'd go to the room naked and wait to get your clothes back in the morning – and this would cause its own problems. The risk of sexual assault and rape was ever present.

Even though I had adapted to prison life to a certain extent, I always dreaded going up into the rooms at night. Nobody looked forward to spending the night in a room full of Thai drug dealers, rapists and perverts.

They were bad enough during the day, but at night they became close to unbearable.

The room where I was held had a small piece of bamboo and a stick. The prisoners used to bang out an all-clear signal every hour on the hour right through the night. The prisoners rotated each night, doing an hour's 'security' and then waking the next man for his stint.

The guards were supposed to walk around and check throughout the prison, but instead they just sat in their chairs and rang a little bell. Every room sent the signal each hour and the guard went back to sleep. If a prisoner fell asleep and missed the signal, he was beaten in the morning. This routine made it almost impossible to sleep.

* * *

The Thai prison system was designed to brutalise the inmates in every way. I cannot over-state this. The authorities installed four one-metre fluorescent tube lights in the cells, which they left on all night. The commandos refused to turn any of them off, and most of us ended up wearing blindfolds to try to get some sleep.

In the beginning I often went for three or four days at a time without sleeping at all. At one stage, I bribed a guard to buy me some sleeping pills. He would only give me one at a time, since if I were to take my life it might be traced back to him, so I'd take the single pill and hope for the best.

But looking back, I now think that more than anything it was the sheer stress of being held in such conditions that made it difficult to sleep for more than a few hours a night.

The other prisoners were also overwhelmingly loud and obnoxious. They would parade around the cell in nothing.

And they would do anything for money. Most begged from everyone else, especially the foreigners, for the money to buy a bag of rice. Sometimes they would need money to gamble or rent a porn magazine.

The gambling and porn created a very violent atmosphere. Gambling led to fights, and in such a small and cramped room that affects everybody. But the porn was worse. I found the whole thing sickening.

Most of the long-term prisoners had lost all their self-respect. They would masturbate constantly in the toilet. There was only a one-metre wall surrounding the toilet, so it was impossible to avoid noticing.

One man masturbating out of a room of 40 might not be so bad, but it was never just one. If someone managed to smuggle a porn magazine into the cell, a queue would form, with maybe 15 or 20 prisoners waiting by the toilet for their turn.

Some didn't even bother going into the toilet. They would just take their penises out and relieve themselves in the middle of the room. When they were finished, they'd either use their t-shirt or a blanket to wipe themselves off.

Others would openly masturbate each other; while others would have sex with other men they called their prison 'wives'. A lot of these men were serving in excess of ten years, and had turned to homosexuality out of desperation.

So for everybody, the threat of gang rape was ever present. I saw men raped many times.

One Thai prisoner I shared a cell with was convicted for raping a child. He was put in my room, and had only been there a few days when we all found out why he was in prison. That night, the room leader gave him a sleeping place beside his own.

Later in the night, he raped him, and continued to rape him every night for a week. The man complained to a guard and was moved. God knows what would have happened if the guard hadn't been sympathetic.

* * *

When I was first sent to prison, I was naive. I didn't look as if I could defend myself or stand up for my rights. But my years inside made me remarkably strong. I eventually changed my image and the way I dealt with people. I shaved my head and got tattoos. After a few months in prison, it was clear to everybody that I would take no nonsense from anyone who gave me trouble.

This made sure that I wasn't raped. I was never sexually assaulted because the other prisoners knew what the consequences of such an action would be. I had changed since I was sent there. I was no longer the slight, straight-laced businessman I once was. I had adapted, and was well able to look after myself.

I was strong, and never resorted to any sexual depravity in order to survive. I blanked it out of my mind as much as possible, but with half the prisoners in some form of fornication or other it wasn't easy.

I've lived among men all my life, and I've worked offshore for months on end, but I'd never seen men act like that before I was in prison. There were times when I wanted to castrate the lot of them, and there were times when it took every ounce of restraint not to get up and kill the bastards.

I found it especially hard when foreigners behaved that way.

I remember one particularly revolting English prisoner called Simon. He had been sent to Chonburi for molesting a woman.

Simon went into a shopping centre and grabbed a sales assistant by the breasts. He got six months.

One night, before anyone had gone to sleep, Simon went to the toilet. He didn't even turn his back, but just sat there and started masturbating. I shouted at him to get a grip of himself and not to behave like the others.

He turned to me grinning and said, 'I can't stop now!'

I'd had enough. I got up and beat the shit out of him.

Simon refused to come into the room the next night. When he explained to the guards why, they all thought it was hilarious. They transferred him to another room.

* * *

Not all of the Thai prisoners were pushovers. There were groups or gangs of Thai inmates who called themselves Samurai. But they had no code and no honour like the real Samurai. They were basically just gangs of thugs who picked on the weaker prisoners, or extorted money from them.

They might not have been real Samurai, but they were dangerous. If you pissed them off, they'd attack. I was particularly cautious around them.

They thought nothing of stabbing rivals with a sharpened toothbrush or spoon, or splitting someone's head open with a plate or even a lump of concrete.

They fought incessantly, and even killed each other over as little as a few cents or anything that they felt caused them to lose face with their friends.

My life was worth more to me than a few cents, so I tried to have as little to do with the Samurai as possible.

Apart from these, most of the fighting that went on was over gambling debts or borrowed money, and some of it was over drugs. But then again, it could be over anything.

I survived by continuing to remind myself that I was the only person I could trust.

I had a few friends in the prison, but by and large I tried not to get too close to anyone. It didn't matter who they were. They were all fucking criminals, and I soon learnt that my fellow prisoners would cheat me in any way they could.

There is one case that springs to mind. Before my arrest, while I was living in Pattaya, an English guy who lived across the road with his boyfriend got to know my wife Nanglung. I'd met him once or twice and he seemed like a nice guy. One day he asked

Right: A colleague and I reporting the con to the tourist police—the department that deals with foreigners. It was at their hands that I would later be brutally tortured for five hours.
© *Andrew Chant*

Left: Leaving Chonburi court. I'd just been found guilty of murder. This was one of the few occasions I was allowed to wear a suit to court, but I was still forced to wear 4 kg shackles on my legs.
© *Andrew Chant*

Working out helped take my mind off things.
© *Author's private collection*

I got some of my aggression out through *muay Thai* kick-boxing while I was in Lard Yao prison.
© *Author's private collection*

Above left: When I was first taken to prison.
© *Andrew Drummond*

Below left: About to be released. I toughened up a lot over the eight-year stretch.
© *Author's private collection*

Below: At Dublin Airport just moments after I arrived home.
Courtesy of the Irish Daily Star on Sunday

Nanglung if he could borrow 5,000 baht until his own money came from England.

My wife asked me if that would be okay.

'If he's really stuck for the money, lend it to him,' I said. So he borrowed the 5,000 baht.

A few weeks passed and, the next thing I knew, he was gone. He'd moved house without saying a word. I felt stupid for trusting him, but that's life.

I'd been in Chonburi Prison for two years when Andrew, or André as he liked to be called, turned up.

He'd been arrested for molesting a young boy, though he claimed he was innocent. Obviously, he was surprised to see me. He knew I'd been arrested, but thought I'd gone to Bangkwang prison in Bangkok.

He apologised about the money.

'Don't worry,' he said. 'Now I'll clear everything.'

He explained that he was just waiting for his embassy to transfer money for him.

I had to help him out with most things in the prison because he didn't know anything or anybody. I got him organised and into a good room, and I got him some credit in the prison shop.

He said that now he knew where I was and the conditions in here, he'd return my 5,000 baht as soon as he got out. He'd also send me food parcels, medicine, books and magazines. Whatever I wanted, I'd get.

A few days later he was gone again, out on bail. I never received a penny of the 5,000 baht, and no food parcels or any of the other things he had promised. In fact, I didn't even get a letter.

What I did get from him was his credit bill in the prison shop – which I had to pay whether I liked it or not. This was typical of the kind of thing that went on.

There is a saying that revenge is a dish best served cold. I met André four years later in another prison. He'd been arrested again for molesting little boys.

I would have kicked his teeth down his throat, but he'd just suffered a stroke and I didn't have the heart to hit him. Amazingly, he asked me for help again.

'Can you help me get moved into your building?' he asked me.

'Not a chance. I don't want you near me,' I said with a shrug.

'Well, maybe you could help me out with some cigarettes and coffee.'

'Fuck off,' I said bluntly, and left the room.

He could fend for himself. It wasn't really revenge; it was poetic justice.

There was no loyalty among any of those criminals. I remember this American guy I used to meet regularly for a few beers and a game of pool. He landed in Chonburi one day. He, like André, told me that he hadn't known where I was being held – or he 'would definitely have visited me'. He said he had been arrested for fighting over his laundry, but was getting out on bail soon.

He was shocked at the state of the place.

'Jesus Christ,' he said. 'How do you survive in this shit?'

He only had the clothes he'd been arrested in and they were filthy, so until they could be washed I gave him some of my own. I bought him a shower bowl, soap, a toothbrush and toothpaste, and a bag of coffee, milk powder and sugar.

He promised to help me in whatever way he could once he got his bail.

A couple of days later his bail came through, and he was gone. Not only did he get out, but the tight bastard took everything with him – my clothes, the shower bowl, a bar of soap, even a half a bag of coffee and sugar. He left nothing. But like André, I'm sure that we will meet again some day.

12

My first few years in Chonburi prison were a nightmare. I was beaten and subjected to utter degradation on a daily basis. I had never felt so low. My Thai wife had stolen my bail money and I could not afford to hire another solicitor.

But as I waited for my trial to conclude formally and for my sentence to be given, my health began to deteriorate. This happened gradually but the effects remain with me to this day.

The rooms we slept in were basically big cages. They had open walls with bars all around.

Parts were covered with mosquito mesh, but other parts weren't.

This was tolerable in the summer, but once the monsoon season came it was a nightmare. The wind and rain beat in mercilessly. A few of us once tried putting up blankets against the bars, but the guards made us take them down immediately. They said they needed to be able to have a clear view on all sides.

In Chonburi, I slept in a room which was designed to hold 20 prisoners, but actually held many more, sleeping sardine-style head to toe.

There wasn't room to fart, never mind sleep. There were no beds – if there were, they could never squeeze the same number of prisoners into a room.

Nobody on the outside really thinks that a prisoner ever goes hungry, especially in this day and age where most prisons around the world serve what could be considered gourmet food. But there was nothing gourmet about the food in a Thai prison. In fact, it didn't even resemble food I'd ever eaten.

We were given what is called *khao dang*, the cheapest grade of rice available. It wasn't washed – just cooked the way it arrived from the farms. In Chonburi, the rice was cooked in huge vats which must never have been cleaned either because, by the time it got to us, it stank.

The fish soup they served was so full of peppers and spices that that's all you'd taste anyway, but God only knows what else was in it.

I was never brave enough to eat the shit they served as food. Anything that smelt that bad couldn't be good for you. I couldn't eat it even if I wanted to.

In fact, the only poor buggers who did eat it were those that didn't have any family or friends outside to visit them or give them a little money.

Most of us bought food from the prison shop. The shop sold white rice, omelettes, chicken, bread and some other things. This was prepared by the guards' wives, mistresses or other family members – but you still got hair, flies, mosquitoes and a few other surprises inside anything you ate. The guards were allowed to sell food to the value of $75 each per day, which meant that in this way, they could make ten times their salaries.

I often went without food for days because I didn't have the money to buy it and I couldn't force myself to eat the shit they provided, but nobody gave a damn. In fact, the prison only prepared food for around 200 people because it was only the very poorest prisoners that would eat it. There was money allotted by the government for food for the whole prison population – but, of course, the guards stole it.

The bad diet I was forced to accept played havoc with my digestive system. I began to lose weight upon entering prison, but I slowly began to lose my health entirely. The fact that there was no medical supervision or care available only quickened my deterioration.

At Chonburi, there was no doctor, just a medic. There was no proper clinic, and no dentist.

My teeth were the first to go. After a few years of the unhealthy atmosphere and awful diet, they got very bad. A dentist did visit Chonburi about once a year. By the time he was due, I was in real pain, so I put my name down to see him.

I went to see him together with another foreigner, Amir. Altogether there were about 500 prisoners going to the dentist that day.

We all had to squat and wait in the yard. Finally, about 12 people arrived in white coats. I thought they looked like students, and my impression turned out to be right.

They started to call out names and people would step up to be treated. But there was no type of examination and no real treatment at all. It soon became obvious that they were only there for one thing – to pull teeth.

The first three or four students gave Novocaine injections. The inmates were then told to stand in line for other students to pull their teeth out.

I looked on in horror. I remember that the students all had rubber gloves and face masks, but there was no real consideration for hygiene. They didn't bring 500 separate syringes. Instead they just dipped the same ones into an alcohol solution and re-used them. It was the same with the teeth pliers.

I looked at the way they operated in disgust. I knew there was no way the pliers could be sterile. I also noticed that the students never once changed their rubber gloves. They were pulling teeth at the rate of one every 30 seconds or thereabouts. When my turn came I refused to go near them and so did Amir.

'Fuck that shit,' I said to him. We walked quickly away, past the students. There was blood everywhere, and bits of teeth were scattered across the yard floor like fallen confetti.

Over the next few months I made dozens of requests to see a proper dentist. They wouldn't let me go out of the prison, even though there was a hospital directly in front of it and I'd only have to walk across the road. They said I was a potential escape risk.

Eventually, probably just so that I'd shut up, the building chief agreed to ask one of the government hospitals to send a dentist.

After looking at my teeth, this dentist said I'd have to have 18 of them removed and I'd have to visit him at the hospital. He said he couldn't pull that many teeth where we were.

When the day came for me to go to the hospital, there was no prison van or car. After all the fuss about security and escape risks and the need for me to be shackled, I went to hospital on the back of a motorcycle.

Don't get me wrong. It wasn't that they'd decided to trust me after all. I still had to wear the chains, so I just threw my leg across the saddle. But it wouldn't have been hard to throttle the guard driving the motorbike and escape. Another prisoner might just have done just that.

I went to the hospital on the back of that motorcycle about ten times. A few times we used one of the guards' pick-ups with me sitting in the back, and we took a taxi a couple of times. I even walked to the hospital twice because there was no transport available. It's a good 30-minute walk to the nearest government hospital, and in 4 kg of shackles that's no joke.

Of course, I had to pay for my own dentures, and my own treatment. The prison should have provided the lot, but they didn't.

* * *

Government regulations in Thailand and the law are actually fairly sound, but the problem is that the Thais never follow them. If they did, life for prisoners would be a lot easier. But they thwart, pervert or ignore the law at every turn.

For example, according to Thai and international law, remand prisoners and convicted prisoners should be segregated. But, in practice, once you enter that gate, you're a convict. There was no inequality in there; they treated everyone like shit.

The only difference was that when a prisoner was convicted, the shackles came off.

Thai law says that 'methods of restraint are never to be used as a form of punishment.' But I'd seen some men with three sets of shackles on their ankles for being caught gambling or using drugs. I saw others with bloody anchor chains on their legs, so heavy that they'd have to half carry, half drag the things around.

But one of the favourites was 'the daisy chain' – usually for those caught in the act of homosexuality or similar, but also for any group caught breaking the rules together. A daisy chain was where all involved – three, five, ten or even more – were all shackled together ankle to ankle.

If one needed to piss, they'd all go; if one needed to shit, they'd all go. They'd have to eat, sleep and shower together – which was bloody difficult, not to mention embarrassing.

The fact that it was illegal to bring a prisoner in front of a court shackled didn't bother these people either. Many people often say to me that judges are not biased when they see shackles. But I disagree.

How can there be a presumption of innocence when prisoners are forced to stand there in chains?

Unlike me, most prisoners didn't know what the law was or what their rights were, and nobody told them.

At one point, I managed to get a copy of the Thai Penitentiary Act from a lawyer. He knew well what the situation inside the prison was but, like all the lawyers I hired, he insisted it wouldn't be good for his career to complain to a judge about it. But I studied the documents he gave me.

As the months passed and I heard nothing about my trial, I gradually came to accept that I would be found guilty. That gave me the courage to start challenging the system from inside. And I became a big problem for the prison. I refused, or should I say, tried to refuse, to be treated like an animal.

After years of being shackled even though I hadn't been convicted of any crime, myself and a Japanese friend, Kim, wrote to Amnesty International and various other human rights groups.

I wrote letters asking them to help have our shackles removed for once and for all.

Our letters were heard and Amnesty advised us to file a case in court to try and get the shackles off.

Word spread quickly and the guards started giving Kim and me extra hassle. The commandos came and told me that if I talked to anybody about what happened inside the prison again, I'd be sorry. They said that when it was over, we'd pay for causing trouble.

Nobody wanted to be seen sitting with us. Everybody was afraid that when the shit hit the fan, they'd also get screwed. It was a very dangerous time but we took the case.

With Amnesty involved, it was listed for hearing in the space of a few months.

The judge couldn't argue with our reasoning and with some human rights lawyers present in court, he was afraid simply to dismiss our case. In the end, he ordered that our shackles be removed immediately. In fact, he ordered all shackles to be removed.

I'd worn shackles for two years, but I knew men who'd worn them for eight. The judgement forced the prison chief to remove shackles from 600 men.

Kim and I were treated like heroes for a day. Even the guards admitted that we had balls. But they now considered us to be troublemakers. One commando went as far as threatening to kill me.

'Oh you think you're special?' he said. 'This is Thailand. You die very easy here.'

It took me a while to realise that at the end of the day, what he said was true, but that didn't deter me.

The success of the case encouraged me to write to every prisoner welfare group in Europe and newspapers in Britain and Ireland. I didn't just ask them to highlight my case; I demanded action.

I started writing letters every day.

One of the people I wrote to was John Mulcahy, the editor of *Phoenix* magazine in Ireland. I remember writing out my entire story for John and thinking that he would never believe a word of it because it was too implausible. But I was wrong.

He did receive the letter and replied. I was shocked. That letter was the first communication that I'd received from anyone in Ireland other than my family. It's hard for me to describe the lifeline this letter represented.

John Mulcahy was entirely non-judgemental and offered to help. As I had been let down so often, I refused to get my spirits up; no one with the exception of Amnesty had done anything practical to assist me.

John proved me wrong. *Phoenix* brought my case to the attention of the Irish public. The publicity immediately produced results.

People started writing to me and sending me parcels of books, medicines and toiletries.

I had long stopped believing in human kindness, but Mulcahy's intervention restored my spirit. The readers of *Phoenix* donated money to an appeal fund which John set up and administered. I can't even begin to explain how this changed my fortunes. Letters arrived from well-wishers every week.

I felt empowered for the first time since I'd been arrested. The letters lifted my spirits; in fact, they saved me. More than anything else, the letters broke the routine. I started to look forward to tomorrow because it usually brought some good news, or an unexpected parcel or letter.

I think I received more post than anyone else.

But in reality it didn't influence my case. I was still faced with the task of seeking justice from what was surely the most corrupt justice system in the world.

13

The mere mention of my trial either sent me into a rage or caused me just to laugh.

It's not hard to see why. The next three or four times I was taken to court, either the prosecutor didn't turn up, or he said he hadn't called a witness for that day.

This repeatedly happened over the course of about nine months. Despite the fact that Thai law states that hearing dates should be no more than 30 days apart, I was only taken to court every three months.

I complained to my appointed lawyer about all the time-wasting antics of the prosecutor.

'The prosecutor is very busy and has many cases,' he said, 'but he could probably find time to come to court and get on with your case, if you're willing to pay him. 100,000 baht should be enough.'

I knew from other men in Chonburi prison that if you paid the prosecutor he could speed up your court dates. I knew some men who'd paid and went to court on average every two weeks. This wasn't considered corruption, because the prosecutor didn't promise to let you off easily. He would only agree to turn up and get on with it. So you actually paid him to prosecute you – but to do it quickly.

One man I knew had been on trial for eight years. The prosecutor listed almost 200 witnesses. Eventually the man paid the prosecutor, who immediately cancelled 20 witnesses. He paid again and the prosecutor cancelled 20 more. And so on.

Getting a quick trial made a great difference. The king of Thailand gave an amnesty every four years on average, by which sentences were commuted. Prisoners like me were only eligible to benefit from an amnesty once we'd been sentenced. But we never knew exactly when the king was going to grant one.

One prisoner I knew was arrested in 1991. There was an amnesty that year but he missed it. There were further amnesties in 1993, 1995 and again in 1999. But he missed them all. If his case had been finished at the time, his 100-year sentence would now be down to around four years. Therefore, bribing a prosecutor to prosecute quickly wasn't as stupid as it sounded.

I didn't have the money and, even if I did, I probably still wouldn't have paid the prosecutor. With O'Connor dead, I knew he had no eyewitnesses. Yet he had refused to close the case, and he'd refused to accept O'Connor's death certificate.

In the end, I decided to write and complain to the president of Chonburi Court. I wrote that the prosecutor had kept me in prison for years, insisting on pursuing a case he couldn't win. I said the prosecutor had no evidence and no witnesses and, so far, had proved nothing.

At the time, it seemed like a good idea. As far as I was concerned, the prosecutor was just playing with my life, and now was asking for money to come to court and do his job.

I asked the president of the court to instruct the prosecutor to get on with my case. If he had any real evidence or witnesses, I said he should bring them to court. If not, let me go.

The next time I went to court, the prosecutor came over to me.

'Why are you trying to make problems for me?' he asked. 'I'm trying to help you!'

When the judge arrived, he told me that if in future I had any problems I could bring them to his attention. He said there was no need to write to the president of the court.

My lawyer at the time said it had been a good idea, but not to do it again. If I did, I'd piss off the judge and the prosecutor.

At this hearing, the prosecutor then introduced the confession the police had forced me to sign. He didn't read it out in court; he didn't ask me if the signature on it was mine. He simply handed it to the judge and said that the accused had confessed to everything at the police station.

As usual, my lawyer just sat there and never opened his mouth or objected. I would have objected myself but the hearing lasted just long enough for the prosecutor to hand the judge the confession. Then the judge was up and out the door with the prosecutor right behind him.

I was sent back to prison.

Six weeks later I was back in court for more of the same. This time, the prosecutor called a police officer. He testified that with the police's amazing powers of deduction they had discovered a murder, caught the murderer, found the murder weapon and secured a confession – all in the space of less than two hours.

The case ended and I was sent back to Chonburi.

I was told weeks later that three other policemen testified in a Bangkok court, which I wasn't allowed to attend. My lawyer went though. He told me that nothing of importance was said.

'Don't worry,' he said. So I worried.

All that remained now was for the prosecutor to make his closing arguments and then the defence would have its turn.

It had taken almost three years to call seven witnesses, and I'd been to court 30 times because witnesses or the prosecutor failed to turn up. On average, most of those hearings only lasted about ten minutes. So in three years, I only had five hours of court time.

As you would expect, there were no closing arguments at each trial. The prosecutor simply stood up, walked over to the judge and handed him O'Connor's statement.

He never read any of it out or showed it to anyone. Once the judge had accepted it, the prosecutor said, 'Oh, and this witness is dead now, Your Honour.'

By this stage, O'Connor had been dead for more than two years and was supposed to have been cancelled as a witness. Now I understood why the prosecutor wouldn't accept the death certificate.

If he didn't admit O'Connor was dead, he could still try to use the man's statement.

When I saw the judge take it from the prosecutor, I was on my feet in seconds demanding that it was illegal to use O'Connor's statement. Nobody could verify the signature. The police could have written it. The prosecutor could have written it for all I knew. He was certainly devious enough.

While I was arguing with my lawyer, the judge and the prosecutor got up and left.

'You should not make a scene in the courtroom!' the lawyer shouted at me. 'It makes it look like you have no manners and no respect for the judge.'

'Being on trial is one thing,' I roared back, 'but having to sit here and get fucked is something else!'

Eventually he said he would talk to the judge just to keep me happy, but the judge would already know that O'Connor's alleged statement couldn't be accepted.

It didn't look that way to me. The judge had accepted it without a word, but there wasn't much I could do now.

* * *

After years of waiting, the day finally arrived for me to testify. I was looking forward to clearing my name. I actually allowed myself to start believing that I would be freed.

I wasn't looking forward to the prosecutor's cross-examination, because I knew he'd try his best to trick me. Some questions you can't answer with a simple 'yes' or 'no'.

But I needn't have worried. The prosecutor didn't turn up. I couldn't believe it. The prosecutor had tried everything to get me convicted, yet now that he had a chance to really grill me, he didn't have a single question that he wanted to ask. How could that be possible?

My lawyer told me not to worry. He said it was normal in Thailand.

The judge didn't seem to think it was strange either. He entered the court, sat down as usual, and opened the hearing without batting an eyelid.

There was no translator in court. This had never really been a problem for them before because any witnesses that had been called were Thai and the judge could understand them.

But now I had to testify and I couldn't speak much Thai. Luckily there was a Thai journalist in court who spoke English. She was eventually asked to translate.

My lawyer asked me to explain what had happened – the original theft, the failure of the police to catch O'Connor, the meeting, how O'Connor had attacked me, and how he had agreed to return the money to me in Bangkok.

The next question was, 'What happened in Bangkok?'

My lawyer skipped the whole car journey with Holdsworth and O'Connor. He didn't mention any fighting or any murder – which was strange, considering that's what I'd come to testify about.

I proceeded to explain how the police had come to O'Connor's apartment and arrested me for trespassing; how I'd explained things and how O'Connor had been arrested instead; how I went willingly with the police to charge O'Connor officially; and how, 14 hours after being arrested, O'Connor had suddenly claimed that I'd killed his bodyguard.

I explained how I'd been beaten and tortured by the Bangkok tourist police until I agreed to sign a statement they had prepared.

The judge just sat there, smiling occasionally but looking bored. He must have heard stories like mine every day. It was normal for the police to beat and torture suspects. I wasn't the first and I won't be the last.

I was never asked whether I'd killed Holdsworth. I was never even asked if I knew him. I was ready to testify how I'd been forced to defend myself against a man attacking me with a knife, but I was never asked.

I confronted my lawyer about this during the lunch break.

'The law is about proof,' he said. 'The prosecutor couldn't even put you at the crime scene. If you testified to being there and said you were involved in a fight, then you'd be doing the prosecutor's job for him. The prosecutor didn't bother to turn up because he knows he doesn't have a case. Don't worry,' he said. 'We'll win the case 100 per cent.'

I wanted to call some witnesses on my own behalf – my wife's brothers who were there when I was attacked, a young supervisor whom I'd called from the police station and some character witnesses. But my lawyer said the young supervisor would be enough.

This witness was called and he testified to my phoning him to tell him what had happened and that I wouldn't be at work the next day. Because no prosecutor came, the judge did the cross-examining but he didn't have many questions to ask.

At that my trial closed. I was told that I would be called back to the court within 45 days to receive the verdict. I expected to be free then.

* * *

That was it. In 45 days I would be going home. It was a long 45 days back inside Chonburi Prison, but that thought kept my spirits high.

When the day came, I was taken to court. I remember feeling excited but also nervous as hell.

My mind was racing. Worst case scenario – if I was found guilty, what would they give me? The most that they could possibly convict me on would be manslaughter, and it was self-defence. Surely those were mitigating circumstances. They couldn't give me more than a few years, could they? They couldn't give me more than I'd already served.

When I arrived in the courtroom, it was empty. No lawyer, no prosecutor and no police.

Nobody – just me, a journalist, and a guard.

A judge I'd never seen before walked in, sat down, saw I was a foreigner and said something in Thai. The journalist later told me what it had been.

'Oh, he's a foreigner,' the judge had said. 'He won't understand Thai, so there's no need to explain.'

Then, in English, he said, 'Found guilty . . . 20 years sentence, reduced by one third because the accused accepted the charge in the police station . . . Now remaining 13 years and four months . . . You can go.'

At that, the judge got up, turned on his heel, and left. I was dumbfounded. My world collapsed there and then.

My lawyer turned up later that afternoon. He already knew the verdict and the sentence. I think he actually knew before I received the news, which is why he didn't come to the courtroom.

I went mad. I broke down. I began shouting and screaming. I was livid. He didn't care. He just shrugged his shoulders and said, 'Never mind, we can appeal.'

'Appeal?' I roared. 'I shouldn't need to fucking appeal! If you'd done your job properly in the first place it would have been impossible to convict me! You let the prosecutor do and say whatever he liked! You never said a fucking word! Is it any wonder I lost? I kept my mouth shut for three years because you assured me you knew what you were doing! You're sacked, useless piece of shit that you are!'

To tell you the truth, I was more annoyed at myself than at him. I should have done something; I should have stood up and objected to the prosecution myself, but I'd trusted him. I was now kicking myself for not knowing better.

When I was returned to prison that night, I immediately contacted the Thai Law Society and asked them to recommend a criminal lawyer. They sent me a list of names and I eventually settled for a Doctor of Law.

I was beyond despair at this point, and had pledged to fight the decision in every way I could. What did I have to lose?

I began to feel less helpless as I prepared for the case. There was always a chance I would be able to correct this dreadful mistake and be freed.

Rather than wait for the lawyers to read up on my case, I wrote out all the points of law I thought should be included in my appeal. I then had it all professionally translated into Thai.

According to Thai law there should have been a minimum of three judges sitting on the bench for my trial. During my trial there was only ever one judge – and not always the same one. I believed this to be illegal.

No translator was present in court during any of my hearings – which is also illegal.

I believed that the judge had acted illegally when he cross-examined me and played the role of both prosecutor and judge. I said that this surely constituted a mistrial.

I also noted that no murder weapon was ever produced in court. The prosecutor only submitted a photocopy of part of a knife, and never even proved it to be the murder weapon.

I stated that O'Connor's alleged testimony should have been stricken from the record. Even the name 'O'Connor' was an alias. It was illegal to use an alias in court. The prosecution still didn't know his real name, which was Mitchel Heath.

And his statement, I'd found out, wasn't even an eyewitness account. The statement only claimed that I told O'Connor I'd just killed his bodyguard – which was hearsay. And because O'Connor had died before my trial opened, nothing that was alleged to have been said by him could be used as evidence to anything.

In total I listed 15 points that I wanted included in my appeal.

This Doctor of Law agreed to include these plus any he himself thought relevant. He said he would write the appeal then bring it to me at the prison to check and sign.

I started to prepare mentally for a new trial.

Although he was recommended by the Thai Law Society, I still didn't trust this lawyer. But he only had to write an appeal, so I didn't think there'd be any problems.

Of course, I was wrong again. On the last day of the time limit to lodge the appeal, he came to see me. He told me he had finished the appeal document and filed it with the court.

He then told me that he didn't think I'd object to anything he'd written, and he'd filed it before coming to visit me to make sure it would be in before the deadline. He'd signed it on my behalf.

He was in a hurry but had left a copy of the appeal with the duty guard. I got the document from the guard as soon as the visit was over.

Not a single point I'd asked to be raised was included.

He didn't object to anything said or done by the prosecutor. He didn't raise the issue of legalities in the way in which my trial was conducted. In fact, he didn't really object to anything.

I'd asked him to say that O'Connor had lied about his name, nationality, occupation and even date of birth, so how could you believe anything he said, if indeed he really had made a statement? The lawyer's version of my point was that O'Connor and I were enemies, so obviously O'Connor would say nothing that might help to acquit me. Not exactly the same thing.

The appeal he wrote and filed was like something you'd expect from a high school student, not a Doctor of Law.

He said he would apply for bail for me, but as a Doctor of Law he wasn't prepared to ask for bail to the tune of only a few thousand dollars. He suggested that I contact my family and ask them to send a quarter of a million.

Needless to say, my family didn't have that sort of money, so there was to be no bail. I was back to square one.

* * *

Almost two years later, I was called to court to hear the verdict. Under the Thai system, a group of five to seven judges review appeal documents in private and make a decision.

The Appeal Court agreed with the decision of the District Court, and upheld the verdict and sentence of 13 years and four months.

Given the weakness of the appeal lodged by my most recent lawyer, it didn't surprise me that I'd lost.

In Thailand, the District Court is only out to convict, and the Appeal Court is basically there for those who throw themselves at the mercy of the court. Having pleaded not guilty in the District Court, they now plead guilty and ask for a reduction in their sentence. I learned that very few people ever win their cases outright.

For those who lose their appeal or are not satisfied with the Appeal Court's decision, there is the *Dika* Court or Supreme Court. This is the highest court in Thailand, and generally speaking it's the best chance anyone has for justice.

Not many people go to the Supreme Court. Money to pay the legal fees is one reason, but the main reason is the time it takes.

On average a trial takes at least three years, an appeal takes another year and a half minimum, and an appeal to the Supreme Court will take about another year. So if you fight your case you're probably going to be in prison for at least five and a half years, but usually more.

The whole system in Thailand is geared towards forcing the accused to accept the charges and plead guilty.

If you accepted the charges in the police station, the court would cut your sentence by a third. If you then pleaded guilty in court your sentence would be reduced by half. Most of the Thai prisoners accepted and pleaded guilty, guilty or not. It made sense – especially for a less serious charge. Would you prefer one or two years in prison as a guilty person, or five and a half trying to prove your innocence?

However, I decided to stay and fight, so it was back to the jungle for me once again.

14

I was fucked in almost every way possible. It was a nightmare. The injustice of it all was depressing, and getting through each day in prison was more so.

Looking back on it now, I realise that the prison authorities operated a divide and conquer policy. They made some of the Thai prisoners into what were called trustees or blueshirts. These prisoners got better food than the regular prisoners, and a few other privileges, like a room to themselves where they could eat or smoke, unlike the rest of us. Most importantly, they got three months' remission on their sentences for every year they worked as blueshirts.

These blueshirts constantly curried favour with the commandos. They cleaned their shoes, washed and ironed their uniforms, and ran to buy them a Coke if they asked. They were the guards' 'boys'.

As a result, they tended to forget that they were also prisoners like the rest of us, and they ordered us around as they pleased. We had no way of knowing which orders really came from the guards and which didn't. They also spied on other prisoners constantly, and reported anything and everything. And, of course, they tried to extort money or cigarettes whenever possible.

But their real job was to be the guards' attack dogs – and they enjoyed their work. If a guard was pissed off at you for any reason, he'd set his dogs on you, and they'd beat you half to death.

In fact, if a guard gave the order, the blueshirts would kill you, and be happy to do it.

One of the other foreigners, Jan from Finland, couldn't or wouldn't count in Thai when the guards did the morning count in each room. A few days later, six or seven of the blueshirts set upon him in the yard, and beat him to within an inch of his life.

Another time, a few foreigners went to shower early, outside the allocated time. A guard nearly had a fit when they disobeyed the prison regulations. So he set his dogs on them. The foreigners ended up with a mixture of broken noses, fractured skulls and smashed faces. One was even stabbed in the arm with a spoon. It's doubtful that they aimed for his arm, so he was very lucky.

The guards themselves didn't actually do very much. There were about four blueshirts for every commando. The blueshirts opened the cells and locked us up again; the blueshirts searched us; the blueshirts checked the mail; the blueshirts controlled the gates in and out of each section of the prison.

The commandos did as little as possible. They arrived in the morning and a prisoner cooked their breakfast. After they ate their fill, they'd go to their factory or office where another prisoner would give them a massage.

After that, they'd take a nap or sleep off last night's hangover. Once they woke, they'd sign the factory ledgers or other paperwork and have lunch. Needless to say, they never paid for any meals or drinks.

In fact, they paid for nothing at all. The prisoners bought everything for them. Every office or factory had a TV for the commandos to watch, which ensured that they did absolutely nothing. They spent the hot afternoons watching TV before their shift ended at 5 p.m.

The commandos rotated for the night shift. If they worked nights it really only meant that they slept in the prison instead of at home. A prisoner would actually make up a bed complete with a mosquito net and fan, and a flask of hot water or coffee standing by.

A lot of the commandos who worked nights would be completely drunk when they arrived at 5 p.m. They would stumble around, helped by the blueshirts. When they came to inspect the cells, some were lucky they could still stand, never mind count the prisoners.

I often saw commandos so drunk they'd pissed themselves. I remember one man in particular who arrived in drunk and started kicking and beating the prisoners just for fun, telling them they should respect him because he was a commando. Ten minutes later, he was slumped in his chair surrounded by a puddle of piss.

At the best of times, the commandos were aggressive, but when they were drunk they'd be downright dangerous. They cracked skulls and broke arms. A lot of them had killed a few prisoners while drunk. I saw them do it.

The most vicious guard I ever encountered was called Paiboon. He was the most sadistic commando in Chonburi. I saw him beat prisoners for hours on end. He used to crawl along the floor, hidden by the low wall, then spring up at the bars to catch people smoking or gambling in the cells.

On the night shift, commandos carry a shotgun. If Paiboon caught someone, he'd call them over to the bars and smash them in the head with the butt of the gun. And they'd still have to report to him in the morning for another beating.

His closest rival as far as downright brutality goes was named Jessada. I saw him beat up prisoners using a two-handed baseball-type swing.

One particular incident stands out in my mind. Some Burmese prisoners had tried to escape from another prison. The next day Jessada called all the Burmese in Chonburi together, and systematically beat the shit out of every one of them. They hadn't done a thing. The escape attempt had happened somewhere miles away, but Jessada kicked the fuck out of them just because they were Burmese. He was a sadistic bastard.

* * *

In all the years I spent in that hell hole, I heard countless stories of the cruelty inflicted on prisoners.

When I heard them at first I didn't believe them. But they were true nonetheless.

I came to learn that prisons in Thailand were run as a business – not by the Thai government, but by the commandos and the prison directors. Everything was designed to make money for the commandos. Whether the prisoners lived or died wasn't important.

For example, every prisoner was given a prison account so that family, friends or an embassy could deposit money for their loved ones to buy food and other necessities. Therefore, the commandos knew which of the prisoners had money, and exactly how much.

They also controlled the prison shop. Inmates had to use coupons to buy anything in the shop, which the commandos also made themselves and sold at a price 10 per cent higher than their value. The food itself was marked up by another 20 per cent. We were a captive market – literally.

The whole place operated on bribery.

If you wanted to move to a different cell, the commandos charged 500 baht to 'assist' you with your request. If you didn't want to work in one of the factories, you had to pay 300 baht a month.

In some buildings the commandos would sell you a shack built out of bits of old wood, where you could sit out of the scorching sun during the day, for 20,000 baht.

Those who wanted to go to the prison school also had to pay the commandos. I spent months in the school learning to speak basic Thai – and paid for it all myself.

A parole application or a request to the king for a royal pardon was supposed to be free. But in practice, it wasn't.

You got nothing in a Thai prison unless you paid for it, and the commandos made a killing. In fact, they seemed to think it was their right to extort money from prisoners.

At Christmas or New Year they'd ask for their tip for being a nice commando. If it was their birthday, they'd also expect a few bob too. I had a commando ask me for money to buy his daughter a birthday present because he was broke. She wasn't my daughter and I really wanted to tell him to go fuck himself, but I ended up giving him the money. It was probably safer.

The thing that made us fear them most, however, was that if they took the notion to do so, they had the power to keep us in here. They had the authority to charge anyone with suspicion of a crime – suspicion of conspiring to escape, suspicion of using drugs, suspicion of gambling, suspicion of fighting.

Any one of these was enough to guarantee at least three months in the *soi* – solitary confinement. Three months is what the law provides for, but they got around that by simply moving a chosen prisoner from one building to another. I know some men who spent over a year in solitary, just moving around like nomads. Every time they were moved they lost some of their possessions – not that any of us had much to start with. It was a cruel regime.

The commando in charge of each building had ultimate power. He gave out the prison rating. These could be either normal prisoner, good prisoner, very good prisoner, or excellent prisoner. There was an interview every six months or so, but only after a case had been finalised.

The rating was important because it affected an inmate's chance of getting parole, and also how much of a reduction in sentence you'd get if the king gave an amnesty. If the commandos charged you with suspicion or anything else, they could cut you down a rating. If they were really pissed off, they'd cut you down two.

This could mean a difference of years in prison. I learned that it was usually best just to pay up and shut up.

* * *

A lot of my fellow prisoners had been jailed for drug running. Drugs were a part of prison life. They were in demand throughout the prison and were big business. Given the state of things, it was little wonder that some people wanted to escape from reality.

Prisoners might smuggle in a few pills or even a little heroin, but over 90 per cent of the drugs were brought in and sold by the guards. The commandos would bring in heroin and mix it up with glucose, baking powder, crushed-up paracetamol or anything else handy.

Heroin in Thailand is usually 98 per cent pure, but by the time it was sold to the prisoners, it was five per cent or less – which meant huge profits for the commandos.

Most of the dealers in Chonburi were Nigerian and they survived by selling drugs for the commandos.

Some of them lived really well from their drug money. And they had plenty of customers.

Most addicts started by snorting a little heroin just for fun or because they were having a particularly bad day. But because of the price, snorting wasn't economical, and eventually they'd shoot it up. A few weeks of that and they'd be hooked. I saw lots of people turn into zombies.

They ended up sharing needles with the other junkies. If they were lucky, they'd only catch hepatitis C, but there was a very good chance they'd get HIV or AIDS. Adding AIDS to the conditions we were forced to live in invariably meant that they didn't last long.

Considering the sheer quantity of heroin sold in the prison, it was impossible to deny that most of it was smuggled in by the commandos. I saw what went on. I knew that no petty thief could stick that amount of heroin down the front of their underwear on the way back from court or a visit. It was the commandos who smuggled it in.

And they were often caught. I know of a commando in Chonburi who was actually caught bringing heroin into the prison but nothing happened to him. He got a slap on the wrist and was transferred to duty on the guard towers. From here, he could still throw his supplies into the yard, and a year later he was back inside the prison doing business as usual.

* * *

The one thing I detested about the commandos most, though, was the way they abused the prisoners' families.

Some of the prisoners' wives or girlfriends would often complain that they didn't have the money to pay off the commandos, so a commando would say to them, 'No problem, I'll take care of him. Don't worry about the money. But you can meet me later and we can go together and have something to eat.'

When they'd meet, the bastards would force a prisoner's wife or girlfriend to have sex with them.

More often than not, the woman would be so afraid of what might happen to her husband if she refused that she'd agree to go. Having used the woman once, the commando would start blackmailing her into being his permanent mistress. Having no respect for a prisoner is one thing, but to do that to his wife or girlfriend is below contempt and downright disgusting.

We were supposed to be the criminals, but the biggest brutes and gangsters in Chonburi were the people who ran the place.

A prison is supposed to be a place of confinement where a convicted person might reflect on his crime and try to rehabilitate himself. There was no such thing as rehabilitation in Chonburi. It was dog eat dog, and only the fittest survived.

Some prisoners left worse than when they first went in; some left as hopeless junkies. Some didn't make it out at all.

In Thailand, they just wanted to punish you. They wanted to punish, hurt and control you, to abuse you and belittle you – and squeeze as much money out of you as they could in the process. Money was their god, and they cheated, stole, conspired, lied, and killed for it.

* * *

I think most people are in denial when they are first sent to prison. I certainly was.

I remember saying to myself, 'This isn't happening,' or, 'They can't do this to me.' But the fact is that they could do it – and they did.

Although the letter-writing campaign lifted my spirits, I still had to battle depression constantly because Chonburi was hell on earth. As you would expect, suicides were common.

Young prisoners often jumped down the four-storey stairwells to kill themselves. The bodies would be left there in a pool of blood until the police came to take photos. Then they lifted them off like a sack of spuds and threw them into the back of a pick-up truck. They didn't believe in using stretchers in Thailand.

I saw dozens of people kill themselves. Some prisoners slashed their wrists and bled to death in the rooms. Others drank rat poison or whatever else they could get their hands on. I know one guy who drank a bottle of resin hardener. I saw three or four climb onto the factory roofs and jump.

The number of suicides never surprised me. What surprised me was that there weren't more.

And yes, there were times when I thought about it myself. But I had four children. I wouldn't want them to grow up thinking their father was a coward who killed himself in prison because he couldn't take it.

15

While I fought off notions of suicide, in October 2000, something happened that posed a real threat to my life. Years of living in squalor and a poor diet collapsed my immune system. I caught tuberculosis.

At first I didn't know what I had, but I knew something was wrong. I was coughing and vomiting uncontrollably and getting really bad chest pains. I couldn't lie down at night without getting stabbing pains in my chest. I also lost about 10 kg in just a few weeks.

My mother had died from heart disease, so naturally I feared that I had developed a similar complaint.

I went to see the medic, who told me that I was probably worrying too much. He just gave me two paracetamol and told me that I would get well soon.

I knew I had something serious, so I went to see the building chief and explained my symptoms. I told him if he didn't get me a doctor I would probably die in his prison, which would give him a lot more paperwork.

Two or three weeks later I was transported to Chonburi Hospital. I was weak and feeble by this stage. I was in constant pain, looked malnourished and could barely walk.

They diagnosed me as having a dangerous strain of TB.

They took blood and sputum tests and the results came back as level three, or chronic TB. It was a relief to know that it wasn't heart disease, but having TB wasn't exactly a joke.

I had to go out to a hospital for chest X-rays. Both my lungs had TB, but my left lung was worse affected.

The prison insisted I give another spit test just to be sure. It's supposed to be done first thing in the morning before you clean your teeth or eat or drink anything, so I was at the office at 6.30 a.m. I had to wait until ten or 11 o'clock before the medic called me for the tests.

The results were the same, plus three, but the medic wouldn't believe me.

'Foreigners don't get TB!' he said. 'You put someone else's spit into your mouth before you come to give the test sample!'

Unlikely as it was, he refused to believe I wasn't tricking him, and refused to give me any medication.

At this stage I'd had enough, and I wrote to the Irish embassy in Kuala Lumpur. I spelled out the seriousness of my situation and told them that if they didn't do something, I was going to die.

As the weeks passed, my condition deteriorated. By January 2001, I'd started coughing up blood, and not just a little blood either.

The embassy wrote to the prison, saying,

'The embassy has been informed that Colin Martin has TB, and you will give him the proper medication until such time as the embassy can arrange his transfer to the prison hospital at Lard Yao Prison in Bangkok.'

By this time, I'd lost over 25 kg and was practically skin and bone. But the letter worked.

I was transferred from Chonburi Prison to Lard Yao on 2 February in a minibus. There were four of us – three Thais going to Chiang Mai and me to Lard Yao in Bangkok. I was accompanied by four commandos armed with Uzi sub-machine-guns at the ready in case any of us should try to escape.

It was a joke. They'd put us all in shackles, so we wouldn't be able to run very far even if we did manage to get away.

I arrived at Lard Yao at eight o'clock on a Friday morning. It lies wall to wall beside two other prisons – Bombat, which is just for drug-related cases, and Bangkok's women's prison.

Lard Yao is massive, holding 9,000 prisoners in total. It was originally built by the Japanese during World War II as a concentration camp. It was later modified a bit, but the original structure remained the same. The atmosphere was bleak and dismal.

On arrival at the hospital section of Lard Yao, I was informed that a doctor wouldn't be available until Monday, so they sent me into the main prison.

Inside Lard Yao there are 14 different sections. When you go into one section, you can only get out if you have a hospital appointment or a visit. Once you're in the belly of the monster, you are trapped.

I found out that different types of prisoner are sent to different buildings. For example, Building One is for the *katoeys*; Building Two is for drug cases and troublemakers; Building Three is for mentally disturbed prisoners and invalids, and so on.

Being a foreigner and therefore supposedly troublesome, I was sent to Building Two, but they wouldn't accept me because I had TB. I was considered too much of a danger. Building One also proved problematic. They said I'd have to cut my moustache before they'd let me in. I refused. Eventually they sent me to Building Three, where the mental patients were kept, but I didn't mind. I was just pleased to put my bags and blankets down.

I stayed in the building over the weekend, then was transferred on Monday to the hospital. They confirmed that I had TB and that my left lung was very bad. They took a number of X-rays which showed the scars where the lining of my lung had ruptured.

I was admitted to the hospital on Friday morning. It was the first time I'd seen a bed in three and a half years – but my joy was to be short-lived. I soon saw what the place was like.

Everybody had to wear pyjamas. The pair I was given had once been white, but were now far from it. They were ripped and covered with bloodstains or vomit stains, and there were stains on the trousers from where other patients had soiled themselves.

The bedclothes weren't much better and God only knows what stains were on them. I later found out that there were cupboards of new and pristine white sheets – but they kept those for when visitors or inspectors came.

The ward I was put into was designated for patients suffering from HIV/AIDS and TB. Most of the 27 patients there had both diseases together.

It was awful. Whatever chance I had of controlling my TB, the others had none. With AIDS, their immune system was destroyed, so the TB slowly killed off their lungs.

The normal medication used to treat TB is a collection of 13 pills plus some vitamins and protein pills. The hospital didn't bother administering any medication to the AIDS patients because they were dying anyway.

It was horrific.

I will never forget what I saw inside Lard Yao hospital. The staff cared nothing about hygiene and even less about the patients. No one was treated with any degree of respect. Every day, people died there without any dignity.

There were some 60 patients with TB in that hospital wing. The staff used to line us up to get our medication each morning. The nurse would dip a cup into a bucket of water and hand out pills – but she used the same cup on every patient. Needless to say, I refused to tolerate this.

I wouldn't eat the food they served either. It came from the AIDS building and was prepared by the AIDS patients. It looked slightly better than the pigswill they served in Chonburi. It contained white rice, at least. But still, I couldn't put it in my mouth. I used to ask myself what if the AIDS patients had cut themselves while making it?

* * *

The hospital wards were run by trustees or patients who'd recovered from their illnesses and stayed on as orderlies. The nurses didn't do anything. They were the same as the commandos back in Chonburi. They spent all day raising chickens, ducks, frogs and fish behind the wards to sell to the inmates. They paid hardly any attention at all to the patients.

The trustees and orderlies did almost everything. They admitted patients, took blood samples, gave medication, and changed drips. Under their care, patients soon found that sickness and disease were the least of their problems.

For a start, the orderlies stole the painkillers and Valium prescribed for seriously ill patients. They sold these at a nice profit to any junkies interested.

The wards had two floors upstairs for those who could still walk, whereas the ground floor was reserved for the near-death or bedridden cases. There was also a morgue – which some of the orderlies used to keep their food fresh.

Like every penal institution in Thailand, there was an ever-present threat of violence. In this case, it was the bedridden patients who were victimised pitilessly by the orderlies.

In the later stages of AIDS, the patients lose control of their bodily functions and often soil themselves. The orderlies were supposed to clean them up, but they were more likely to beat the shit out of these patients, throw them out of the bed and drag them – or, more often than not, make them crawl – to the bathroom to clean themselves.

Those who couldn't walk because they were too close to death were dragged screaming and propped up in a corner, where they were hosed down. It was horrific.

I saw some patients who had meningitis and lost control of their bodily functions. They would moan and cry out in pain involuntarily. The orderlies often beat them just for making noise. They hated the patients.

My most sickening memory is of the orderlies placing bets on how long it took a patient to die.

The longer I stayed there the worse it got. Some of the chronically ill patients pleaded with me to help them. They feared they would be killed in their sleep. At first I thought they were crazy, but I soon found out that this danger was very real.

In the three days I spent there, three patients died in the night. I believe they were murdered. One orderly told me that he thought nothing of killing someone to speed things up.

The killings never came to light because the orderlies threatened and tortured the other patients so they wouldn't dare say anything.

There was nothing I could do. If you're bedridden or seriously ill you're entirely at the mercy of the orderlies. And I was near death.

I was supposed to stay in that hospital for a couple of months, but after three days, I'd seen enough. I was afraid that I would be murdered. On the third day, I went to see the head doctor to demand that they let me out of the hospital section. I just wanted out of there.

Eventually he agreed, but said that I'd have to wear a face mask at all times once back in the real prison building. I didn't mind. If that's what it took to get me out of the hospital, I'd have agreed to wear a space suit.

* * *

I was sent back to a cell in the main prison filled with TB victims. As in the hospital, there were men with both TB and AIDS together with those with just TB.

For a recovery or treatment room, it was stinking and unhygienic. It was dirty, with scrawls of graffiti all over the walls. The plaster was all cracked and falling off. There were bits of lino in places, but the rest was just bare concrete floor.

Reading some of the graffiti, it was obvious that the room hadn't been painted in over 25 years. Any money that had been allocated for repairs or paint had been stolen by the commandos – just like everything else.

John Mulcahy in Dublin had continued to campaign for my release. We wrote to each other every week. He had been instrumental in highlighting my situation and, I believe, had played a part in inducing the Irish embassy to take action as regards getting me moved to Lard Yao.

In one of our many letters I told him about the condition of this so-called recovery room. I asked John if he could send me some money from the appeal fund to redecorate the recovery room.

It wasn't a matter of wanting to do it. I had to. I was going to be in the TB room for at least six months. Trying to cure anything in those conditions would have been impossible.

John sent me the money, and I bribed one of the commandos into buying a couple of gallons of disinfectant. Together with the other patients, we scrubbed down the walls, the floor and the toilet area.

Next, I bought sand and cement and repaired the walls. Two days later, I bought paint and brushes and we painted the whole room. I also bought new lino for the floor and paid to have the toilet fixed.

When we had finished, it looked like a normal hospital room. I felt elated. Being able to help those less fortunate than myself was an added benefit and gave me a new will to live.

You might ask how I managed to get the materials to repair the cell into the prison. That was easy.

The commandos made a request to the prison's correction department for the materials needed. The correction department sent the money. The commandos bought what was needed, then charged me again for the same amount. They could have made repairs to the cell at any time by making a simple request to the correction department – but there'd be no profit in that. Instead, they waited until they found a way to make money.

When it was all finished, it felt like I'd moved into a hotel. It cost a lot of money, but I hadn't really had much choice.

After six months my TB was still at level one. The doctor said I'd have to be readmitted to the hospital where I'd undergo further treatment. This would involve daily injections of a strong antibiotic called streptomycin.

When I was called to the office and told that I'd have to go back to the hospital, I refused. I told the building chief that I'd already seen what the hospital was like. I said he could lock me up in solitary or do whatever he wanted, but I wasn't going back to stay in that hospital. If he sent me back, I told him, I'd have him charged with attempted murder.

He talked with the doctor and they agreed that I could walk to the hospital every day.

So for the next 60 days I walked over and got my injections. That was 60 days, and 60 injections.

I would get a shot in the right cheek one day, and in the left cheek the next. The injections actually caused a lot of pain. They were like tetanus shots and went straight to the bone, giving muscle cramps and spasms. That's why they liked to admit patients to hospital. Most people don't want to walk after getting a shot like that, but I didn't care. As far as I was concerned, I was going to suffer whether I was in or out of the hospital.

The injections were all given by a prisoner working in the hospital. I never even saw a nurse or a doctor.

Some days the guy giving the injections would say, 'Maybe today it will hurt a little bit.' There was something about the way he made the comment that irritated me. It sounded odd.

A week later, I found out that he'd been re-using the needles and selling the new ones to the junkies for 250 baht each.

Thankfully, after the 60 injections, I was no longer positive. I still had TB but I was told that it would cure itself. I still had to take 15 or 20 pills for breakfast every morning, but I was happy to be finished with the needles.

The next problem I had to deal with was my weight. I'd lost over 25 kg and I needed to pile on the pounds if I was to regain my health properly.

At the time, I was still finding it hard to eat. I'd feel hungry but, once I smelled the food, I didn't want it any more. I'd have to pinch my nose to force a few spoonfuls of soup or something down into my stomach. I'd sit, nearly in tears, forcing myself to eat just one more spoon.

I'd buy baby formula, as it was easy to get down and was full of vitamins and minerals. I drank tons of the stuff. Instead of trying to eat three large meals a day, I decided to eat six or seven small ones. It worked, and my weight eventually climbed up to 60 kg.

Putting on weight isn't cheap in a Thai prison, but I'd started to receive food parcels from people in Ireland who'd read about my situation in the newspapers. The food I received helped me to rebuild myself.

Although I was still physically ill, I felt better within myself. I had accepted what had happened and had dealt with the situation. I stopped getting angry and began to work the system. My change in attitude also coincided with a visit from John Mulcahy.

I greeted him like a long lost friend; his visit, more than any other, boosted my spirits. I felt confident that something positive was going to happen, although I was not quite sure what.

It took a year and a half for me to cure the TB, and then another year to get my weight back up to normal. If that medic in Chonburi Prison had given me the medication when he should have, I could probably have been cured in three months.

16

Although Lard Yao was a much less severe prison than Chonburi, the commandos were as violent and dangerous. They loved to inflict pain and to humiliate the prisoners, and often engaged in brutal violence, rape and even murder.

They were thugs and murdering bastards. They hated prisoners and never missed an opportunity to dispense punishment. As in Chonburi, the blueshirts followed their lead. This resulted in prisoners having to face danger at every turn.

I recall one particular incident which happened shortly after I arrived there. At the time, I was still receiving medical treatment for my tuberculosis.

One of the guards told me that someone from the Irish embassy had come to visit. This was nothing unusual. I left my cell and headed towards the main gate which lay close to the visiting room.

As I strolled over, a blueshirt named Joe asked me where I was going.

'Embassy visit,' I said.

'Which embassy?' he asked.

He was standing there with the visit permission slip explaining who, what, where and when – all in Thai.

'Can't you read? It's in your own language!'

He gave me a sullen look, and told me to go and sit down and wait for the official to arrive. When the time came, he called me.

We got to the gate leading out to the visit area, and he pushed me through.

'When you come back I'm going to kick your ass!' he hissed.

He was of a slight build. I was now feeling a lot better and decided that I wasn't going to be intimidated any more.

I turned around and walked towards him.

'Why wait?' I said. 'Do it now.'

He looked surprised, and I thought it must be because I was calling his bluff. He mumbled something and walked off ahead of me.

When we got to the visiting room, we came upon another blueshirt unlocking the door.

'Put this prick in there,' he said.

'You're the prick, Joe, not me,' I replied.

I thought nothing more of the incident. I had a good meeting with the embassy clerk and didn't give any more thought to the matter. I considered Joe to be just an arrogant arsehole.

My trouble started once the visit ended. When I got back to the prison gate, I was met by 20 or more blueshirts.

At first I didn't even think about them. They had a lot of freedom and would often congregate in groups like that. They just told me to sit on the bench and wait. Then Joe turned up and, quick as a flash, I was surrounded.

He accused me of insulting him and demanded that I apologise in front of his friends. Joe took a few steps forward and started pounding his palm menacingly with his baton.

'If you were a man, you'd apologise,' he said.

'I'm more man than you'll ever be,' I snapped. 'And I'm not fucking apologising!'

He kicked me in the ribs.

I tried to get up off the bench but the other blueshirts held me back. This wasn't hard; I was still pretty lean because of the TB. In fact, most people who met me took me for a junkie.

Joe knew I was weak and kept barking at me like a dog.

'You have to apologise! You have to say you're sorry!'

I refused.

'Say you're sorry? What is this schoolboy shite?'

I told Joe again that I wasn't going to apologise for anything, and tried to get up. He kicked me again, but this time I was ready.

I caught his leg and flipped him over and as soon as he hit the ground I hit him.

That was my mistake. The other 20 blueshirts jumped on me at once. It was a real free-for-all, and they hit and kicked me willy-nilly.

When it was over, I scrambled to my feet. I saw a commando sitting about 20 yards away. I can still see him sitting there, just smiling.

'You're supposed to stop this shit, you bastard, not just fucking sit there!' I cried.

He laughed dryly.

'Go away, foreigner,' he replied. 'Go back to your building.'

The blueshirts hadn't really beaten me that badly; they'd given me mostly cuts and bruises. I felt lucky, in fact, because they hadn't used their batons.

But before setting up to lynch me they had obviously asked the commando for permission. My guess is that he told them they could kick me around a little, but not hit me with their batons. After all, he wouldn't want too much blood on his nice clean floor.

I complained to the embassy – not because I was hurt, but because I'd have to go through that same gate each day to go to the hospital. I said that I didn't want to have to fight the blueshirts every day. They in turn sent a letter to the prison.

I don't know what they said, but it worked.

Days later, the Assistant Director called me to his office. He explained that the commando in charge on the day was new and didn't know all the regulations yet. If I filed my complaint his career as a commando would be finished. He asked if I would let the matter drop and accept his word that it would never happen again.

I had no choice. I could have made a formal complaint, but it would probably have got me killed. So I told him that if he removed Joe from the gate, I'd let it go.

You might think I was the loser but I had won that battle; I'd stood up to the prison authorities and more or less got away with it.

* * *

That same month, the commandos beat to death eight prisoners in Bombat Prison, which adjoins Lard Yao.

The eight prisoners had tried to escape. They had smashed a commando over the head while he was sleeping and made a run for the wall. Once the alarm was raised, the blueshirts went after them.

While the other prisoners were counted and locked inside the factories, the blueshirts caught the escapees and dragged them over to the waiting commandos.

The commandos picked one at a time, and beat and kicked them until each was unconscious. While one was being beaten, they made the rest stand and watch until it was their turn.

Knowing what was coming next, some of the escapees made a desperate attempt to get away, and somehow managed to climb the wall that separated the prisons.

I saw the whole thing unfold from my cell. I watched two of them scurry around the trees that grow between the prisons.

One jumped down into Lard Yao, but he soon realised that one of our blueshirts had spotted him, and disappeared back over the wall.

Eventually, the blueshirts in Bombat got hold of them all and they were dragged off to be beaten.

The commandos weren't content with just beating the shit out of them once, though. While they were lying there unconscious, the commandos threw water at their faces to revive them. One commando decided that water wouldn't do the job, and urinated on the prisoners instead as they lay there, unconscious.

When the prisoners awoke, the commandos started attacking again. They beat them mercilessly, and this time they continued until all eight were dead.

Even though none of the commandos carried a gun, the news reports claimed the eight prisoners had been shot while trying to escape. They had got around this problem by shooting all eight after they died.

On the newsreel, all the bodies were covered, the bloodstains showing clearly against the white sheets. Most had injuries to the torso, but some had multiple bloodstains to the face and head area.

Unbelievably, the commandos still weren't satisfied. After they had murdered the prisoners, they went and gathered all the prisoners who had been friends with the eight men, or had ever shared a room with them. Each of these men was handcuffed or tied up, and beaten.

In fact, they followed that practice in every Thai prison. If someone ever escaped or tried to flee, they beat and punished everyone that knew him.

Only two months after that incident, the commandos in Lard Yao beat a half-Thai, half-Chinese prisoner to death in Building Two.

The prisoner had stuck a nail in the wall to hang his coat or bag on. A commando told him to take it down, but he told the commando to fuck off. The commando hit him, and immediately let his blueshirts loose on the inmate.

They were, as usual, a little over-zealous, and the prisoner had to be taken to the hospital for stitches and a broken arm. When they brought him back from the hospital, he was put into leg irons and dragged off to solitary. Soon he was paid a visit in solitary by the commando and his henchmen. They beat the poor bastard until he passed out.

About an hour or so later, the other men in solitary noticed that he was having trouble breathing, and called out to the guard on duty.

By the time the commando got off his arse and came to the cell, it was too late. The man had died.

This case was not unique.

Another time, during a routine search by the blueshirts, a Nigerian prisoner was caught with about 30 g of heroin, which he quickly swallowed. They should have taken him to the hospital and made him sick or used a stomach pump to retrieve the drugs. But the commandos had a better idea:

'Let's beat it out of him.'

Maybe they thought that if they kicked him hard enough, he'd throw up the heroin without wasting time by going to the hospital. It didn't work that way though.

The beating they administered caused the bag of heroin to burst in his stomach. The man died, and it was explained away as a junkie overdosing.

Nobody really knows the total number of prisoners maimed or killed by the commandos, because nobody cares.

I saw prisoners left with brain damage or crippled for life. I lived with one man who was left paralysed down his left side because he had been beaten so badly.

Other men were left with permanent limps. Throughout the prison, and the Thai justice system as a whole, there were men who weren't so lucky, and didn't survive the beatings they received.

Life meant nothing to the commandos, and if you pissed them off or gave them enough reason, they'd kill you in a minute and then laugh about it. For all prisoners, violence or the threat of violence was never far away. It was just something we had to live with.

Anyone who visited me passed remarks when they saw the commandos and their bamboo batons and nightsticks. Most people thought the weapons were only for show, but they were not.

The commandos made sure that visitors saw very little. Thorough care was taken to make sure visitors never saw the real face of a Thai prison.

* * *

Despite the ever-present threat of violence in Lard Yao, my health continued to improve. I had exhausted virtually every avenue of legal appeal without any real success but I just got on with life. I suppose you could say that I had come to accept what had happened and that I would have to serve out my full sentence.

When I realised that there was no use in fighting the system I just adapted to it, though I managed never to become institutionalised.

Sure, I continued to campaign for my release with the help of John Mulcahy, but privately I accepted my fate and looked forward to the day when I would be freed.

I had no other choice.

When I regained my health, I decided to get fit. I had never been much of a sportsman but now I decided to train. If nothing else, it would take my mind off things.

My new found desire to become fit coincided with a decision by the Thai prison authorities to hold its own version of the 2002 World Cup.

Each prison was told to compile a team which represented a participating country.

I volunteered to join in to have some fun but it didn't take me long to realise that the whole competition was a fraud.

When the idea was first suggested, the prison authorities sought sponsorship from large companies and the government. In order to attract investment, they invited representatives from various TV stations and journalists, a few embassy officials and some other VIPs.

Pepsi then agreed to sponsor the event to the tune of five million baht. Once they were on board, other companies donated money for a chance to get free

PR. When the sponsorship money was in place, the Minister for Justice agreed to open the event.

When I say the event was a fraud, I don't mean to say we never played football. We did – but it wasn't anything like most people were led to believe.

The prison authorities refused to buy the team kits and provide us with the football shoes that had been provided for by the sponsorship money.

The commandos pocketed the money instead and forced us to pay for everything ourselves. The prisoners were the ones who bought the team kits, the socks, boots and everything else. We even paid for the footballs.

The guards made a killing. They even charged the inmates who wanted to watch the competition and cheer their team on. The inmates were forced to pay 200 baht for this privilege.

The sponsorship money was stolen almost wholesale. All we got was a couple of free glasses of Pepsi, a towel and a couple of pairs of underpants. As usual, the prison and the commandos kept or stole the money for themselves.

They did the same thing six months later when they announced that they would start a Thai kick-boxing programme in the prison.

I became fascinated by the sport which the locals called *muay Thai*. This kind of boxing was a vigorous martial art that had developed over the past 2000 years. It used to be called *pahuyuth* a couple of hundred years ago, but had mutated into a modern sport.

Many Europeans, even in the martial arts world, did not know about *muay Thai*; very few people taught it, because it not only involves punching and kicking but the use of your elbows and knees.

The conditioning regimen used to prepare fighters was legendary for its intensity and rigour. Fighters became hardened to an incredible degree. Getting kicked in the shin by a *muay Thai* fighter is often likened to being hit by a baseball bat.

I couldn't wait to get involved. But the guards were wary of the whole idea. I think they worried that we might start beating them up, or at least make the blueshirts think twice about assaulting us the way they did now. But their objections, thankfully, went unheeded by the authorities.

The prison chief told us that participants would be trained by a professional trainer, and those who made the grade would be allowed go and fight in one of the local stadiums. Naturally, all training equipment would be provided by the prison.

When I heard this I knew exactly what was going on: it was another money-making racket.

The prison had raised sponsorship money from some of the boxing stadiums outside, partly to help the prisoners, but also to promote the sport.

This didn't deter me. As far as I was concerned, they could keep all the money as long as I got to train.

About 15 foreigners signed up to fight. On the first day a trainer did come to Lard Yao, watched a couple of us perform kicks and took the time to show us a few basic moves.

The Assistant Director and the commandos watched the training session.

But that was the last I ever saw of the trainer. I presume he lost interest when the Assistant Director refused to pay him for his time.

I was undeterred. I made some discreet enquiries about the sport. I heard that some of the Thai prisoners in my building used to be champions before being sent to prison. True enough, as it turned out, there were a few.

Rather than abandon my plans, I and two others asked these prisoners to train us. They agreed, and under their guidance we learned how to fight.

The training regime we followed was rigorous, exhausting and punishing. And I loved it.

I learned the basic techniques first. The training involved learning to use the hands, elbows, kicks and knees to punch and kick your opponent.

Though the high kicks looked spectacular during competitions, I quickly learned that the elbows and the knees were the most damaging weapons used by fighters. Sometimes they were even deadly.

Two *muay Thai* techniques became my favourites. These were the Thai low kick and the Thai roundhouse kick.

I would practise these for hours and hours. The low kick uses a circular movement of the entire body to kick an opponent's leg with the upper part of the shin. When not correctly defended against, this technique often ends the fight. After a few low kicks, the opponent cannot stand any more.

The Thai roundhouse kick was also unique as far as I was concerned. This kick is carried out with a straight leg and the entire body rotating from the hip.

I learned that almost all techniques in *muay Thai* used the entire body movement, rotating the hip with each kick, punch and block. As a result, most techniques are slower, but much more powerful than boxing or karate.

Although we had no proper equipment, all we could do really was run, skip and box a little, but it hardened us. I found the training exhilarating. It took my mind off my situation and gave me a purpose in prison.

The commandos watched me train from a distance. Other prisoners avoided getting into rows with the three of us because we looked muscular and fit. The change in my physical appearance was dramatic.

I went from being someone who could be mistaken for a heroin addict to someone who might just as easily pass for a bodybuilder. I became very muscular and flexible.

Eventually, we made our own kick-pad out of blankets and an old sack. We trained on this for months, but every time we kicked or punched it, we damaged it.

By this time, a number of Irish people living in Bangkok had become involved in the campaign to have me freed. I won't name them because they wish to remain anonymous. They often came to the prison with parcels of food and medicines. These welcome visitors came every week. They brought fruit, drinks and food to the prison, which helped me keep mind, body and soul together.

They also acted as a point of contact between me and John Mulcahy at times when one of us needed to get an urgent message to the other.

I was reluctant to ask these people for anything, given everything that they were doing for me, but I eventually caved in. After many sore fists and bruised knees, I sent word to my benefactors asking if they would help me to buy some proper boxing equipment.

I was prepared to fight but wasn't prepared to step into a ring only half-trained. They agreed and bought everything – gloves, head guards, kicking pads, punching pads and even jock straps.

I then paid 5,000 baht to build a frame to hang a punch-bag on.

With the proper equipment I began to excel as a fighter. My technique got better and my senses became more acute. I trained morning, noon and night.

Muay Thai is usually taught in a boxing camp that is run by a family. Students warm up by running three to four miles a day, they spar in the afternoon and practise their techniques. They also get Thai massage to alleviate injuries and relax their muscles after a fight.

In prison, we had no such luxuries. We trained all day. If we got hurt, we fought harder so as not to get hurt again.

While I was just happy to train and fight, I learned that winning *muay Thai* fighting competitions was all about technique. To produce a good score, fighters were urged to show their technique and how it had a visible effect on their opponent. It was not the number or variety of *muay Thai* techniques used that judges looked for, but their effectiveness.

Judges also looked to award the fight to the strongest fighter. I prepared for competition bearing this in mind. As far as I was concerned, I might as well have been training for the world title.

But, as I expected, the inter-prison championship turned out to be nothing more than another scam for the prison.

Although we had trained and were ready to face down any adversary they put in front of us, when it came to the competition, no one went out to a proper boxing stadium. Instead, they erected a makeshift ring at the front of the prison where fights took place.

A few prisoners were brought from other prisons to come and fight but, as with everything else, the commandos refused to let us fight unless we paid them. They also charged the inmates to watch the few fights that were staged and stole every penny they raised in sponsorship.

When I found out they were charging the inmates to watch the fight, I lost all interest. While I would turn a blind eye to being personally ripped off by the commandos, it didn't feel right when I knew the guards were making money from the poorer inmates. I couldn't stop them doing this, but there was no way I was going to facilitate them.

17

When I wasn't fighting in the ring, I continued to fight my way through the courts. After my appeal had been rejected, I was offered the chance to pay $80,000 or 4,000,000 baht and win my case.

It wasn't said explicitly, but the money I was asked for would be used to bribe the legal fraternity and offset the legal fees.

At the time, I couldn't afford it, so I declined and hired yet another lawyer, whom I instructed to appeal my case to the Supreme Court. This was a risky decision; few murder appeals win on points of law.

Nevertheless, this time I put together a solid appeal and hoped that the judges in the Supreme Court would at least review my case properly.

The points I raised were more or less the same as those I had wanted to submit to the Court of Criminal Appeal. The difference this time was that my lawyer was reputable, efficient and honest. This made sure that the case didn't take long to come to court.

Just ten months later, on 31 July 2003, I was summonsed to the Supreme Court in Bangkok along with 20 others.

I was told that it would be a very formal hearing. In preparation for what I believed would be a very formal court appearance, I asked if I could wear a suit, and was told that I could have worn one at every appearance if I wanted. No one had told me this, and it seemed no one had told anybody else either. The prison guard who escorted me said that it was the first time he'd seen an inmate wear a suit in 33 years.

When I arrived at the court, there was only one judge, who sat at a bench reading a stack of papers. He called out a prisoner's name and then read the verdict.

I listened attentively to the other cases as they were called. I felt sure I'd be going home. Despite all my previous disappointments, I'd never felt so sure that I would soon be free.

Case after case was dismissed; the judge seemed to rule in favour of each defendant. Even if he didn't overturn a conviction, he'd reduce the sentence by half or a third.

I listened in amazement. I had never seen anything like this in Thailand. This felt like the kind of court where at last I might get some justice. This was the first judge I'd encountered who seemed competent.

I recall that I was the only foreigner there that day and my case was called last. When I heard my name mentioned, I was overcome by nerves.

As I got to my feet, my legs went wobbly. I waited for the verdict.

The judge began to read the judgement. He never looked at me directly but maintained his concentration on delivering the judgement.

He said, 'There is no real evidence and no real witnesses against the accused, and the prosecutor's case is not very sound.'

I thought I was hearing things. For the first time since my arrest, I actually believed that I was going to win.

The judge continued, 'However, the testimony of Mr O'Connor is very damning. Therefore, the court *believes* that the accused is guilty.

'The court feels sorry for the accused knowing that he has lost his business, his home and a large amount of money at the hands of Mr O'Connor.

'The accused is an educated man and has caused no trouble while he has been in prison. His claim of torture by police is not believed. The police would have no reason to torture him.'

I stood there in silence. I looked at the judge, not really knowing how to react or what to do. I just stood there. I felt nothing. I was lost.

'The court feels sorry for the accused's family and considers the sentence imposed to be too high. The court now reduces that sentence to ten years.'

'All rise,' said the clerk.

That was it; there was nothing more I could do. Everything had been in vain. I had taken my case to the highest court in Thailand and lost; there was nowhere left for me to go.

I could have asked the Thai government to transfer me back home to Ireland after I'd served four years, but I had decided to stay and fight my case in the belief that eventually I could win.

I wanted the Thai courts to acquit me, not just to release me. I wanted to clear my name.

Looking back, it's now obvious that I never really had a chance. Of all the lawyers I hired, not one tried to fight my case properly.

What I eventually learned was that I should never have trusted any of them.

As I stood alone in the courtroom that afternoon, lost in a language I could not speak, surrounded by customs I really didn't understand, I felt a remarkable sense of calm.

I said nothing to the judge as I left. I didn't even acknowledge his presence.

I believed, as my lawyer did, that the Supreme Court wanted to release me, but were afraid I'd sue for false imprisonment. If the Supreme Court had overturned my conviction, it would have been an official acknowledgement that the previous courts had made mistakes.

I think the Supreme Court reduced my sentence because they simply couldn't justify keeping me in prison for much longer.

But the reduction was really just a token gesture. You may think that 13 years and four months is a long sentence in Thailand but this is not the case.

Life imprisonment in Thailand is 100 years, and the average sentence imposed by a Thai court is usually

25 years. If the Supreme Court had really thought I was guilty, they'd have increased the sentence.

So when they reduced my sentence from 13 years to ten, it didn't mean that much to me. I'd already served half of the 13 years. I knew an amnesty was due in a year or so, and my sentence would probably be reduced by half.

In that case, a three-year reduction wouldn't actually change anything. If my name was included in the amnesty I'd be out in a year. The Supreme Court knew this as I did.

I had fought the prosecution through three courts in a battle that took over six years to lose. As I stood there, I thought about the six-year journey through hell that I had travelled. I felt a huge wave of stress and frustration at the whole thing.

I thought back over everything that had happened. Despite everything – the beatings, the torture and the squalor of prison life – the true hopelessness of my situation struck me. I thought of my children back in Ireland, my young son Brendan struggling to survive in Bangkok and my own brothers and sisters. I was only thankful that my own mother and father weren't alive to suffer the anguish of seeing their son in a Thai jail.

I believed the verdict of the Supreme Court was illegal, but I accepted it because I was powerless to do anything about it.

It all made sense to me now. I didn't feel despondent or heartbroken, but strangely relaxed.

I returned to the hell hole that was Lard Yao that same evening, as if nothing out of the ordinary had happened. I suppose you could say nothing had.

* * *

With the passing of the New Year in 2004, I resigned myself to serving out the remainder of my sentence. I felt this was the best course of action. I had served over seven years in jail and I'd experienced more defeats, heartbreak and torture than most people ever experience in their whole life.

I tried not to allow myself to sink into a real depression, and decided to concentrate my mind on anything but the Thai justice system.

Despite my glum outlook on life, there was a general feeling of optimism in Lard Yao that January. We were told that the king of Thailand would grant an amnesty the following August in honour of the queen's birthday, which celebrated her sixth life cycle. In Thailand, every 12 years is a life cycle, and Thai people mark it as a special occasion in their lives.

Under these amnesties, prisoners are granted a reduction in their sentences up to 50 per cent, according to their prison rating. That is, unless they're convicted of an offence that Thai people consider particularly despicable – like drug dealing, killing a parent or a monk, or an extremely vicious murder.

If I was one of those given the privilege of a 50 per cent reduction, I calculated that I would be freed immediately.

But I refused to allow myself even to think for a moment that I would be among the chosen few. Past experiences had taught me better.

I also knew it was pot luck as to whether the king would actually grant an amnesty or not. There were no guarantees.

After the initial rush of excitement the news of the amnesty generated, prison life returned to normal.

Some of the inmates didn't care much about the amnesty anyway. Many of them knew they would never be released because of the crimes they committed.

The hundreds of inmates convicted for drug-related offences knew they hadn't a hope. The king of Thailand was known to be totally against drug dealers and had never once granted a reduction to a convicted dealer.

These prisoners knew they were going nowhere in a hurry and often became a threat to the rest of us for this very reason. They resented those who had a good chance at getting out, and would go out of their way to get others into trouble with the commandos. It is astonishing how people react to other people's good fortunes.

I watched as the drug dealers turned into a separate population within the prison population. They came to blame everyone else for the situation they found themselves in.

They'd start fights with the better-behaved prisoners over nothing, and began to cause trouble left, right and centre. In this atmosphere, I had to watch my back and avoid trouble at all costs. If a drug dealer started giving me hassle, I walked the other way. If the commandos wanted to pick a fight, I just ignored them.

I had no other choice.

I'd come too far now to risk ruining my chance of getting out. Looking back, I think it is really surprising what the human body can endure if it has to. At the time, I recall feeling as mentally and physically strong as the day I was first arrested. Yet I was under terrible pressure and stress.

I had bad days when the frustration really got to me but I would say to myself, 'Tomorrow is a whole new day. Who knows what it will bring?'

One thing was for sure: things could only get better.

* * *

That August was a long time coming. The days passed slowly. The only thing that made life worth living was the boxing. Life inside the prison changed as everybody in Lard Yao waited anxiously for news of the amnesty.

In fact, we talked about nothing else. At that point in my life I took stock. I listed the three most harrowing things that happened to me. The first was my arrest and torture, the second was the TB, and the third was living with the constant threat that the commandos might murder or maim me like they had so many of my fellow inmates.

These stark realities were always on my mind, but I couldn't help becoming like the others. I day-dreamed about the amnesty and sweet freedom.

Everyone was the same. We became obsessed with the amnesty. They even started a lottery on which inmates would be freed and whose sentences would be reduced.

As the time drew nearer, the prisoners found it difficult to sleep with the excitement, including myself.

Our day of reckoning finally came on August 12 when Prime Minister Thaksin and the Minister for Justice visited Lard Yao to announce the amnesty formally. This was a major event for the inmates.

Television crews and journalists poured into the prison complex to film the first batch of prisoners being released.

That day, we were all locked up but allowed to watch an old television to hear the news. It was nerve-racking stuff for everyone.

I imagine it was the same in every prison across Thailand, where over 300,000 prisoners waited to see what the amnesty would hold for them.

No one said a word as the Prime Minister spoke, though no one was interested in anything he was saying. Eventually, at around 12.30 p.m., Thaksin formally announced the amnesty.

Without hesitation, he delivered the terms, saying, 'All normal-type cases will have their sentences reduced by half.'

The whole prison erupted in screams and applause. Everybody shouted and cheered with delight.

We were going home. The tears rolled down my cheeks and I wept openly. The nightmare was over.

I knew I'd have to wait up to 60 days for the prison authorities to process the paperwork, but that didn't matter. I was going home. I dreamed about seeing my children, holding their hands as we walked and talked. I wondered what they would look like and how they would react to me finally being home.

It wasn't until two days after the announcement that the official documents were posted on the prison notice board.

My heart sank as I read the small print. I learned that the actual amnesty held nothing for me.

The document read, 'Reduction in sentence of one half for all cases of theft, fraud, robbery, murder etc, EXCEPT fraud concerning or via a bank, EXCEPT all cases concerning the loss of life, EXCEPT all cases where it is the second offence committed by the prisoner. For those cases mentioned as exempt from the one-half reduction, they will be entitled to receive a maximum reduction of a third in their sentences, depending on their prison rating.'

My case had involved the loss of life, so I was not entitled to remission. My king's amnesty therefore depended on the ratings afforded to me by the commandos.

This was disastrous. Ratings were only given after a case was finalised. Because I had fought my case and made two appeals, I had only received two prison ratings, and the last one was only good to very good, not the excellent that would qualify me for the one-third reduction. I was only entitled to a reduction of a quarter. That was two and a half years off my ten-year sentence.

My reduced sentence was seven and a half years, which meant I had six months left to serve. I wouldn't be going home after all.

I felt completely gutted, but I had been knocked back like this before, so I didn't get visibly upset. The commandos, blueshirts and drug dealers were gloating over our disappointment, and I wouldn't give them the satisfaction of seeing how upset I was.

I looked on the bright side. I would be out in another six months no matter what, but for some men it would be years more before they'd be free.

* * *

My official release date after the amnesty was set at 18 January 2005. After I cursed at the thoughts of spending another Christmas and New Year in that miserable hell hole I got on with life once more. Only this time, the end was in sight.

As the time got closer, I couldn't believe I was actually going to be free. I hadn't been able to sleep for weeks. I was an emotional wreck.

I actually became afraid to go home. I started asking myself questions like what would I do once I landed? Where was I going to live? I didn't have a house or a flat, and I couldn't sleep on someone's couch for the rest of my life.

I didn't want people coming up to me in bars and asking me what it was really like in a Thai prison. I didn't want people to buy me drinks so they could gossip with their cronies. I didn't want people pointing at me in the street.

My fears got worse as I thought about it. What would I live on? How would I buy food? How would I buy clothes? I didn't have anything of my own; I didn't even own a pair of shoes. In prison, I was only allowed to wear flip-flops.

I asked myself questions about literally everything. How would I find a job? What about a girlfriend or a wife? Who would want to get involved with an unemployed ex-murderer?

I had been treated like an animal for so long I had almost begun to believe I was one. I couldn't believe I'd survived seven and a half years in that hell hole.

* * *

When the day finally came, a guard came to me and told me I was going to be deported. I was to gather my possessions and prepare to leave.

He said I would be taken to the Siriacha Immigration Detention Centre until my travel arrangements were finalised.

It was actually happening. I couldn't believe it.

Everyone except the guards was happy for me. I hastily collected what belongings I had and gave my friends all the sports equipment I'd bought. I gave away most of my clothing, my bedding, and my radio.

I went around and said goodbye to everyone. People hugged me. I felt terrible for them. I knew that many of them would never get to see this day; they would die in this stinking hell hole.

After that it was just a matter of collecting what little money I had in my prison account and then signing the release papers.

I was marched by two commandos to the front gate. In all the years that I'd spent there, I had never been to this part of the prison. I glanced over my shoulder as I left the prison complex. It was a surreal experience that has remained with me to this day.

Through a window, I could see the outside world. Bangkok hadn't changed in the almost eight years I'd spent inside. The city was still the same.

* * *

The Siriacha Police were waiting for me with handcuffs, but after talking to the prison guards they decided they wouldn't need to handcuff me. I wasn't going to give them any problems.

It felt fantastic finally to walk the last 50 yards and out into the fresh air of real life and freedom. Well, almost freedom.

I was marched to a pick-up truck parked outside the front gate and ordered to sit into the back seat.

This was the last time I'd get to see the imposing structure of Lard Yao. It was almost tranquil to look at from the outside. Only the inmates knew the horror and squalor of the inside.

Once I got into the jeep, the guards got in and sat beside me. We drove a short distance to the immigration office in Siriacha where I was processed.

I was told that I would have to spend the night there in a cell with 12 others. These were all Cambodians who'd entered Thailand illegally to work. This didn't bother me. The police cell was like a hotel compared to some of the places I'd recently lived in.

The next morning, I was taken in the back of a pick-up truck back to the Immigration Detention

Centre. The jeep drove leisurely along the winding back streets. When I got there, it was as if they had wrenched freedom from my grasp. It was just like Lard Yao.

I was processed yet again and pushed into an overcrowded cell. There was no room to stand, there were no beds, and the whole place stank of shit.

Everybody slept on the floor. Each room had a room leader and you had to pay him for a place to sleep and the use of a couple of old blankets.

When I objected to the conditions, the immigration staff went mad. After a brief argument with them, I gave up. I knew the score. They would hold me there for months if I got on the wrong side of the guards. I bit my lip and said nothing. There was no point.

When I began to look around, I was very surprised to see three guys from Cambodia whom I'd known in Lard Yao. They'd been released back in August with the amnesty but they didn't have the money for their air fares home, so they were now stuck in the Immigration Detention Centre until they could somehow raise it.

Luckily for me, the money for my air fare wasn't a problem thanks to John Mulcahy and *Phoenix*.

I didn't sleep much that night. The place reminded me of Chonburi Prison. There were remarkable similarities between the two places; they were both overcrowded hell holes.

The next morning, Trudy Goodfield from the Irish consulate came to see me and told me that she had arranged my ticket home. Trudy knew her way around Bangkok and had been helpful in the past.

She said there would be no problems. She said she'd bought my ticket and faxed the airline to confirm that there'd be no problems.

I was taken to Bangkok's Don Muang Airport by an immigration officer on 26 January.

In typical Thai style, he had the handcuffs ready, but offered not to cuff me for a bribe of 500 baht. The Thai police were determined to get every penny I had right to the very end. This smart bastard explained that if I arrived at the check-in desk handcuffed to him, the airline would view me as dangerous and there would be a good chance that I wouldn't be allowed to board the flight.

I didn't know whether he was telling the truth or lying but I wasn't willing to take the chance. I handed him the money.

Once at the airport, I was handed over to the immigration officials based there. On that day there were six people brought for deportation – three Chinese women, one Pakistani man, one Colombian and myself. Downstairs, the holding cells were packed with foreigners still waiting on money for their tickets home.

Thailand is corrupt to the core. People facing deportation have to pay for their own fare home, and they are sent back to jail if they can't.

With 30 minutes left to flight time, I was approached by one of the guards and told that I wouldn't be allowed to check in or travel on any flight. He said the airline had said they wouldn't accept deportees.

That was it. I lost my temper and demanded that I be allowed speak to the flight attendants.

If I didn't get a flight I'd have to go back to the detention centre – for days, weeks or months.

All I wanted was to go home. Now, with freedom so close, I couldn't bear to think that it might be taken away from me again.

The only thing to do was to try a different airline. I had a little money in my pocket, but I knew it wouldn't be enough for another ticket. After all I'd been through there was no way that I was going back to that shit hole of a detention centre without trying.

Some of my Irish friends from Bangkok had come to the airport to see me off, so I borrowed some money from them.

I bribed the guard into accompanying me to the flight desks. I tried airline after airline but not one would accept deportees.

Finally, I was told that Thai Airways might take me. With three minutes to final call I dashed over and begged the flight attendant to sell me a ticket.

She said no at first, but agreed to help when I spoke to her in Thai. I bought a ticket, dashed back to check in and then raced off to the boarding gate.

Once I went through the gate I didn't even look back. I rushed onto the plane that would take me home.

The guard tried to extort money from me right till the end. As he let me go, he asked me for money for his daughter. It was at this point that I told him to fuck off. I handed my passport to the immigration control and never looked back. I was going home.

18

I decided that I wouldn't go straight home to my family. If I did that, I figured, I'd get the bends. It would be just too much for me to handle. Instead, I would take some time to myself and just get used to being free.

I made my way to a bar in Shepherds Bush run by a friend who had written to me while I was in prison. Her name was Margaret, and she'd been good enough to send me food parcels and cards while I was in Bangkok. She agreed to let me stay with her for a few days.

When I walked into the bar, I was dumbfounded. The barmaid asked me what I'd like to drink but I just couldn't answer. I looked around me but I hardly recognised any of the stuff on the shelves. Everything had changed so much in the years I'd been away.

'Just give me a pint of lager,' I said.

The barmaid just stood there looking at me, until I eventually pointed at the Stella tap.

I couldn't believe how good it tasted. I'd never enjoyed a pint so much. Anything we'd had to drink in prison was always lukewarm and usually dirty. I wasn't used to the feeling of being really refreshed by food or drink, and it came as a surprise to feel the cold liquid hit my stomach. This was the first beer I'd had since I'd sat laughing with the police captain in his office eight years previously, just before I was taken to be tortured.

Margaret gave me a good meal and I went to bed early. I was exhausted, but I couldn't sleep at first. I was staying in the bedroom of Margaret's teenage daughter, who had just moved away to university. The room was huge, papered all over in pink, and the bed was big and soft, with a fluffy duvet. I couldn't imagine anything further away from the stinking cell I had shared with 60 criminals. It made my head reel. How could I fit into this world of comfort after what I'd been through, what I'd seen? How could I ever become a normal, happy person again? With these thoughts whirling around in my mind, I eventually fell into a deep, exhausted sleep.

When I awoke it was afternoon. After I'd showered and eaten, I decided to go into the city and do a little sightseeing and shopping. Of course, I had no clothes except the shorts, and t-shirt I'd worn in prison and a few items I'd borrowed from one of the people who'd been helping me out there. I got myself kitted out with a decent shirt and trousers, and bought a pair of shoes. The shoes actually hurt my feet – it was a long time since I'd been able to wear anything except flip-flops or cheap trainers, and at first I felt a little confined.

After I'd made myself presentable, the first thing I did was visit one of the agencies that had helped me. I wanted to thank them in person. They were surprised to see me, and told me that no one they had helped had ever come to see them before. They asked me all sorts of questions, including what they could do for the boys over there, and what they could send that would make life a little easier. I wanted to forget the whole thing, and didn't particularly enjoy going over the whole experience again, but the kindness of people like these was sometimes the only thing that kept me going in there. I didn't want to forget about them just because I had my freedom. That wouldn't be right or fair – and believe it or not, I still believed in justice.

One of the strangest things I experienced at that time was walking through the London crowds. I was used to having people pressing in on me all the time, and constantly having to watch my back. When I found myself surrounded by Londoners on a crowded street, in a lift or even in a queue in a shop, my guard went up automatically. I felt very nervous and my instinct was just to get out of there.

At one point that afternoon I was in a gift shop trying to choose presents to bring home to my family. The shop was small and cluttered, and all of a sudden a group of tourists rushed in. They were all shouting in a language I didn't understand, pushing each other and laughing. I was forcibly reminded of the cells at Chonburi, at the time when I knew no one and couldn't speak any Thai. For one second, the horror rushed back into my mind and overwhelmed me. I left my basket of gifts on the shop floor and made for the door as quickly as I could.

All in all, though, it was fantastic to be free. I stayed about a week in London, and I made up my mind to enjoy myself. In the evenings I would go for a drink in the bar with Margaret and her friends, and sometimes I would just wander around the pubs and nightclubs, just getting used to being able to do what I wanted, and talking to ordinary decent people who didn't want to screw money out of me.

As I say, I'd decided to enjoy myself, and I did get pretty drunk on one or two of those nights. I think I needed to. It was a way to let out all the tension, to try to deal with the enormous change in my life.

One night I found myself in the bar of a hotel. I fell in with a group of five or six people who were staying there. They wanted to know about me, what I did, where I was from and so on – so I told them I had just been released from Lard Yao prison. All of a sudden everybody started buying me pints, and the next thing I knew, I was well and truly pissed.

Everyone in the group was nice, but there was one young woman I was getting on with particularly well. Her name was Kate, and she was beautiful, with blonde hair and big, blue eyes. I found I could really talk to her, and she seemed to understand me. She didn't just want to hear the gory details of what went on in prison, and it was a relief not to be asked about them. We soon found ourselves separated from the rest of the group and deep in conversation.

I hadn't allowed myself to think about women at all when I was in prison. If I had, I'd have gone mad or ended up losing my self-control like Simon or the other scumbags in there. But now, a beautiful young woman was showing real interest in me. I could hardly believe it.

At the end of the night, she invited me up to her room.

I woke up the next morning with a pounding head. Kate was already dressed and getting ready to leave. She was going back home that morning to the north of England. I'd realised that we were both in London for only a short time, and besides, I wasn't ready for a relationship, but I definitely wasn't sorry I'd met her. After all, I'd been celibate for eight years. I wasn't about to say no when a gorgeous blonde invited me up to her hotel room.

I gave her a kiss on the cheek before she left, then she went her way and I went mine.

* * *

I needed London. Eight years' worth of anger and distress was pent up in my mind and my body. A few mad nights had helped me to let it all out. But after a week or so, I was ready to go back to my real life.

Some friends collected me from London and brought me back to Dublin, to help ease the transition into my new world. I arrived in Dublin at 7.30 p.m. on 31 January 2005. My brother Tommy was to drive down and pick me up. I couldn't wait to see him again, but I was nervous at the same time. I didn't know how he'd react to me after so long, or whether we could still have the close relationship we once did.

It was almost an anti-climax arriving home. My friends had deliberately kept my arrival quiet, so there was no throng of press journalists – just a solitary photographer knew about my arrival and he finished taking his shots fairly quickly. We sat and waited for Tommy to arrive. After an hour there was no sign of him, but we decided to stay another while longer. Forty minutes later I figured that he must have changed his mind, so we left.

I stayed in Dublin that night. Everything was still strange to me, right down to the smallest things like upholstered furniture, knobs on the doors and even having knives and forks to eat with. I'd been using my hands for so long I could only fumble clumsily with proper cutlery. It would take me ages to eat a meal, and I'm sure there were people who thought I was a real clown when they saw me miss my mouth and drop food all over the place. But even though everything I had known so well was now unfamiliar to me, it was clear that things had changed a hell of a lot.

I was glad to see that the country had become a lot more multi-cultural than it was before I left. I saw people from just about every part of the world on the streets of Dublin, it seemed. Every single person had a sleek little mobile phone, which looked a million miles away from the brick-like things which had been available to only a few people when I was last in Ireland.

I checked into a hotel for the rest of the night and rang Tommy as soon as I settled in. He had just arrived back from Dublin Airport – empty handed! He had gone to the airport to collect me as arranged, but he didn't recognise me. I didn't realise I had changed so much. I knew I was no broader and stronger looking, and my shaved head now replaced the balding patch that I once sported, but I figured my brother would recognise me. He had expected me to be alone, so when he saw me with a man and woman he assumed he must have been mistaken. The following morning, my friend drove me to Dundalk to meet Tommy, and this time, there was no case of mistaken identity. We hugged each other so tightly and tried to erase the years that had separated us. It was truly wonderful seeing him again and for the first time since being released, I started to really unwind and let the remaining tension leave me.

We walked about the town, where everything in general seemed to have become a lot more sophisticated. Tommy told me that the White Oaks pub where I used to drink in my home town was now an upmarket restaurant. Then there was the euro. It was going to take a while to get used to a new currency. For a long time I took a pocket calculator wherever I went.

Despite all these changes, despite the fact that very little was familiar to me now, I really felt like I was coming back to where I belonged. After years of displacement, I was finally home.

I stayed with Tommy when I went back to my home town the next day. The first thing I did was to go and see my children. Jason is now 17, Carl is 13 and Nicole is now 12. I had thought that I might never see them again, so I was over the moon actually to be back in their company. We had been in constant contact while

I was in jail; they wrote to me all the time, so I hadn't been totally cut off. But I was delighted to see how much they'd grown, how they'd turned into young adults. I was so proud of them all.

They were a little reserved with me at first, but after a while it was just as it always had been. I had just missed Nicole's birthday, so I took her shopping and treated her to some new clothes. I would take them all for ice cream or to the cinema, or we would watch movies together at home. Just spending time with them made me feel unbelievably lucky. If there's one good thing that has come out of my prison experience, it's that I probably appreciate my family even more than I would have if I hadn't had to live without them for eight years. I'll never ever take them for granted.

I've never lied to them about what happened to me. That wouldn't be right or fair to them. But I don't think they fully understand the horror of what went on in there. How could they? It's hard enough for most adults to absorb, even if they know the whole story. I've asked their mother to read this book first, and then decide if they should be allowed to see it. But my feeling is that the sooner all of us forget about it, the better.

It took me a while to pull my head together, but I think I've adjusted fairly well to life on the outside. I've got myself a place to live near where my children and their mother live, and I started working as a welder recently. During a radio interview, a former employer of mine rang in to say that I was one of the best welders that had ever worked for him, and that I could have a job with him whenever I wanted it. I soon took him up on his offer

I still write to a few of the guys I was friends with in Lard Yao. I know how much a letter means to the prisoners, so I've sworn to myself that I won't forget them. I try not to rub it in – if I've just been for a steak dinner I tactfully leave it out of my letter – but they're always keen to know what I'm up to and how I'm getting on.

As best I can, I have been trying to block out the memory of what happened to me in Thailand. I try not to think about it. But that's more easily said than done, and something – a smell, a chance remark or something as vague as the expression in someone's face – will always bring the whole ordeal up in my mind when I least expect it.

Sometimes I still feel like going out drinking like I did when I was in London. It's easy for me to see why so many people who have been through a trauma like mine become alcoholics. Alcohol will drive out the memories, even if only for a while. But no matter how much you drink, they will always come back eventually – in your thoughts and in your dreams. The Bangkok Hilton will always be with me.

I'll never be the same person as I was before I went to Thailand either. I'm a changed man. I spent close to eight years in a Thai prison. That's bound to fuck you up to some degree, no matter how strong you are. I witnessed things that no one should ever have to see; I was forced to do things no one should have to do.

One of the things that disturbed me the most was that my eyes were opened to the ability of one human being to inflict cruelty and brutality upon another. It was beyond any normal person's comprehension. But the single most disgusting, the most appalling and saddest thing I encountered, was indifference. The indifference of the guards, the indifference of the system, the indifference of Thailand's population and the world's public to injustice. It was an indifference that's a disgrace to the human race.

I've written this book to try and put a stop to this indifference. There are thousands like me – innocent people subjected to unspeakable suffering in Thailand.

When I was dying in that stinking hell hole, I didn't want pity – I wanted justice. But before the system can be changed, its horror must be acknowledged.

The kind of suffering I went through is hard for most people to imagine. I've written this book so you don't have to imagine it. Most people will find it hard to take in; some won't even believe it. But it's all true, and I've written it so that the abominable brutality and injustice people like me are being subjected to every day will be known and acknowledged. I've told my story for you. I've told my story so that you can look hell in the eye.

Epilogue

There is nothing new about the conditions and brutality in the Thai prison system. It's been going on for years and it's been reported for years, yet nothing has really changed. Most people in the world have at least heard about some of the horror stories coming out of Thailand. The Thai government and public are fully aware of what goes on behind these walls, but nobody seems to care.

It's surprising just how quickly you can lose your friends when you've been charged with murder. Almost no one from my home town bothered to write to me. The town council were more interested in chip vans and where they should be allowed to park.

For Irish prisoners in Thailand and elsewhere around the world, there is the Irish Commission for Prisoners Overseas (ICPO). They're a charity organisation that tries to help Irish men and women incarcerated in foreign countries. Unfortunately they don't have a big enough budget to offer financial assistance, but they still do whatever they can and will push the Foreign Affairs department for action as much as possible.

They also write and send cards to prisoners. They have a pen friend scheme too. All I could ever say was that I loved them all and I'd be home as soon as I could. It wasn't much of an answer, but it's the only answer I had.

Now I'm out of that hole we'll have to try and recover some of the years we've lost.

My wife Nanglung has offered to sell me my son Brendan. Of course, I have no intention of buying my child, but the embassy is due to issue him with a passport. Eventually he'll come to Ireland to live with me, and we can try to live as a family. How much my children have actually been affected by all this is impossible to tell, but children are strong. My hope is that they'll forget quickly, and we can get on with our lives.

Acknowledgements

Many kind-hearted people in Ireland and elsewhere gave me support, and it meant the world to me.

My greatest supporter was John Mulcahy at *Phoenix*. He wrote a number of articles in his magazine to highlight my case. An appeal fund was launched by *Phoenix* which enabled me buy food and cover my legal costs.

The support the appeal received was fantastic and, to be honest, I couldn't have survived without it. People from all over Ireland seem to have sent in a few quid. It was great to know that if I needed money for food or medicine I only had to ask and John would send it. No more worrying where my next meal would come from really lifted a weight from my shoulders. I owe a debt that I could never repay to all the people of Ireland who had the heart to help me, even though they'd probably never even heard of me before.

A Ms Lily Byrne, whom I knew only vaguely, wrote offering to help in any way she could. She arranged a petition demanding that the Irish Foreign Affairs department look into my case.

I received a letter from Dr Liam O'Gorman who is a member of Amnesty International in Ireland. Dr O'Gorman tried to use any of his contacts to put pressure on the Irish government to help me and he wrote numerous letters himself. We became good friends, and he sent me some money and a parcel of medical supplies that would cure anything from a headache to hairy palms.

Journalist John Mooney wrote a few articles in his paper, reprinted the *Phoenix* appeal and included my name and address at the prison so that people could write to me directly. He also donated money himself to my appeal fund. He even took the time to come and visit me.

Elizabeth O'Neill of *Magill* also made the trip out to Thailand. *Magill* printed articles I'd written under the title *Letters from Bangkok*, and they too donated money to my appeal. I had various other Irish journalists write or visit me if they were in Thailand, but John Mulcahy, John Mooney and Elizabeth O'Neill are the ones that really stand out.

I also got a visit from time to time from Dr Dan Breen. He's an Irish professor at one of the universities in Thailand. Dr Breen is also a member of the Thai Union of Civil Liberties and he gave me advice and tried to help me with my case.

There were always a lot of missionaries visiting too. I didn't go to any of the visits with the bible bashers. I didn't need anyone to tell me about Jesus. I had learnt a long time ago that nobody was going to save me.

A priest called Father Oliver and an Irish nun working in Bangkok, Sister Louise Horgan, were the only ones who didn't try to stuff religion down my throat. I was always pleased to see them. Sister Louise might be getting on a bit, but she always made me laugh – something we really needed in prison.

I also had visits from people passing through Thailand on holiday. Some had read about me before they came over. Obviously, a few were nervous about coming and some weren't sure if I'd want to be visited by strangers, but they still came. For people to take time out from a holiday they'd just paid a fortune for to come and visit a prisoner meant a lot to the men behind bars. It might be the only visit they ever got, or the only friendly face they ever saw. We did get the odd thrill seeker who only wanted to know the gory details, but 99 per cent were genuinely interested in our welfare and shocked at the conditions we were forced to live in. Some would leave a little money or buy us some fruit in the prison shop at the front of the prison (these visits were always known as 'banana visits').

The food they bought I always shared with the other guys who didn't have much, and when they'd get a banana visit they'd share with me. It's the way we survived. Most of the men would share what little they had, because being selfish doesn't pay in the end.

I had visits from people of many nationalities. Two beautiful Danish girls stick out in my mind, as they came back to visit me two or three times, and two beautiful English girls, Tanya Cook and Alisha, who visited and then sent postcards to cheer me up.

Some of the Irish bars in Pattaya and Bangkok took collections from time to time to raise a little money to help when it was needed. I felt very lucky.

My pen friend Ann did a great job of cheering me up. I wrote a lot of letters in prison and have been lucky to make such good friends – Helen, Miriam and Colin, Arthur, Eddie, Martha, and John L.

I received letters and cards and also food parcels, some on a regular basis, from Helen, Martha, Tom, Liam, Margaret, John and Paddy, to name just a few. Unfortunately, some of the people who wrote or sent parcels didn't include a return address, so to some people I never will get the chance to say thank you.

I also received letters and parcels from Margaret Shiels in London. She's the proprietor of the Coningham Arms, an Irish bar in Shepherd's Bush where I used to drink when I was working in London at the age of 18.

My ex-wife Paula and my three children wrote to me regularly. Although it can be hard explaining to your children where you are and why, I never lied to them about it. That wouldn't be right or fair to them. It was very hard for me, though, when my daughter asked, 'Daddy, when are you coming home?'

How do you explain to your children that you're innocent but they still lock you up? How do you explain about appeals and verdicts and constitutional courts, or amnesty from the king?

All I could ever say was that I loved them all and I'd be home as soon as I could. It wasn't much of an answer, but it's the only answer I had.

Now I'm out of that hole we'll have to try and recover some of the years we've lost.